ULTIMATE BASS FISHING LIBRARY

ADVANCED BASS FISHING SKILLS:

BEST LURES,
TECHNIQUES
AND PRESENTATIONS

MONTGOMERY, ALABAMA

INTRODUCTION

D O YOU KNOW the most common mistake anglers make when rigging soft plastics? Do you know what the "clear" favorite hard bait is for Kevin VanDam, one of the world's best bass fishermen? Do you know the best lure to employ so that your kids really enjoy their fishing trips with you?

Read this book and you'll learn the answers to those questions and probably most others you might have regarding lures and techniques used for bass fishing.

For more than 30 years, we've learned how to catch America's favorite sportfish from the best — Roland Martin, Bill Dance, Larry Nixon, Rick Clunn, Ken Cook, Shaw Grigsby, David Fritts, Jay Yelas, Mark Menendez and other B.A.S.S. touring pros. And we've shared that information with you in BASSMASTER Magazine.

In this book, you'll find the best of the best from the past decade, including some of the latest trends and tactics.

Early into the 21st century, tournament bass fishing is more competitive than ever before. If an angler is to succeed, he can't just take a bait out of its package, tie it on, and expect to finish in the money. By experimenting with casts, retrieves and tackle, he has to learn how to make that lure catch fish when most others who are using it are not. In long, tiring days of practice, he has to find ways to make it productive during times and seasons when many of his peers would not think of throwing it. During long drives from one tournament site to another, he has to think of ways to modify his baits so they will give bass a different look and, thus, be more appealing.

Sometimes he succeeds. Sometimes he does not. Fortunately for the nation's millions of bass fishermen, the tournament pro almost always is generous with what he has learned when he does succeed.

In these pages, you will learn how to be more versatile with your spinnerbaits, lizards, grubs, freak baits, tubes, craws, jigs, spoons, and lipless crankbaits.

You will learn how to modify your Spooks, soft jerkbaits, and deep divers.

You will learn how to take advantage of the "eyeball" factor when rigging the newest generation of plastic crawfish.

You will learn which topwater baits require the slowest presentations.

You will learn how to make a superdeep crankbait work for you instead of against you. And you will learn much, much more.

If you're a tournament fisherman, this knowledge just might give you a decided edge over your less educated competitors. If you like to fish for fun, it should heighten your pleasure by helping you, your friends and family members catch more and bigger bass.

One way or another, if you are a bass angler, this book is for you.

Enjoy.

Copyright 2003 by B.A.S.S.

Published in 2003 by B.A.S.S.
5845 Carmichael Road
Montgomery, AL 36117

Editor-In-Chief:
Dave Precht

Editor:
James Hall

Managing Editor:
Robert Montgomery

Editorial Assistant:
Althea Goodyear

Art Director:
Rick Reed

Designers:
Laurie Willis, Leah Cochrane, Bill Gantt

Illustrators:
Chris Armstrong, Shannon Barnes,
Lenny McPherson, John Manfredi,
Jeffrey K. Preg

Photography Manager:
Gerald Crawford

Contributing Writers:
Chris Altman, Richard Alden Bean,
Wade L. Bourne, Paul Cañada,
Mark Hicks, Michael Jones,
Robert Montgomery, John Neporadny Jr.,
Steve Price, Louie Stout, Tim Tucker,
Don Wirth

Contributing Photographers:
Chris Altman, Richard Alden Bean,
Wade L. Bourne, Paul Cañada, Soc Clay,
Gerald Crawford, Mark Hicks,
Michael Jones, Bill Lindner,
Robert Montgomery, John Neporadny Jr.,
Dave Precht, Steve Price, Louie Stout,
Tim Tucker, Don Wirth

Copy Editors:
Laura Harris, Debbie Salter

Manufacturing Manager:
Bill Holmes

Marketing:
Betsy B. Peters

**Vice President &
General Manager, B.A.S.S:**
Dean Kessel

Printed on American paper by
Quebecor World

ISBN 1-890280-00-3

THE BEND of the rod in early morning light defines an angler's passion. The contents of *Advanced Bass Fishing Skills* will improve the frequency of such bends, adding success to each day on the water.

CONTENTS

TECHNIQUES

The perfect pitch
lands a lure quietly
and precisely on target . . .

TARGETING BASS:

Understanding lure presentation and strike zones

ONE OF THE FIRST, and most crucial lessons Larry Nixon learned in his competitive fishing career was the importance of lure presentation. The combination of casting style, retrieve and lure placement determine whether a bass will ignore a lure or attack it.

IT'S A HOT, windless June day on Florida's Lake Tohopekaliga, but the milfoil is fresh and green, and Larry Nixon has been catching bass with a plastic worm around isolated clumps of the vegetation. He's not catching enough, however, and someone else wins the tournament — with a spinnerbait, no less.

More than 20 years later, Nixon still remembers the lesson he learned that week.

"It was the first time I realized just how crucial casting and lure presentation can be," says the four time MegaBucks winner and 1983 BASS

Listening To The Bass

A strike, whether or not it results in a hookup, can reveal important facts about the mood of the bass, but you have to pay attention. By noting where the lure landed and where the bass intercepted it, you can determine how actively the fish are feeding, where they are positioned and how best to retrieve the lure.

cover bass are likely to be using, how they are positioned in the cover, and the depth they are holding.

"The mood of the bass basically determines your lure choice and type of presentation," he continues. "The trouble is, you learn the answer only by making a lot of different lure presentations, such as fast, slow, stop-and-go, or whatever. Are the fish feeding well enough for a fast retrieve, or are they hiding in the cover and demanding a slow, precise pitching/flipping presentation?

"The key is recognizing what bass are telling you, and the quicker you learn what mood they're in, the faster you can refine your tactics to take advantage of the situation."

ANALYZING MOODS

The very first strike of the day can provide a major clue, and it can also give initial information on how bass are positioned in cover — which, in turn, tells you where and how to cast.

"If the bass are feeding well, you can cast beyond a target and reel past it, and they'll strike," Nixon advises, "but as every fisherman knows, bass are not feeding most of the time. Fortunately, when they aren't feeding, you can still excite them enough to get a reaction strike, such as with a fast moving spinnerbait."

Here again, it is critical to recognize exactly where and when a strike occurs, notes the

Masters Classic champion. "The winner couldn't catch a fish if he moved his spinnerbait more than 2 feet. The bass were tight to cover and had a small strike zone, so every cast he made had to be very specific."

With that thought in mind, says Nixon, the very first question he tries to answer each day he's on the water is, "What mood are the bass in?" That is, how aggressive are the bass, and how far will they move to intercept a lure?

In addition, Nixon wants to know the type of

LARRY NIXON HAS learned that strike zones expand and contract according to the seasons. In the fall, bass typically are shallow and are feeding actively in anticipation of winter. They'll chase down fast moving lures like spinnerbaits and crankbaits. In midwinter, the strike zone shrinks, requiring a more vertical presentation with spoons and jigs.

Arkansas pro. Getting a hit the moment the lure touches the water, for example, does not necessarily mean the bass are actively feeding. Instead, it might mean you have to present your lure exactly where the bass are located because their strike zone is very small.

"Over the years, I've found that probably nine times out of 10, the strike zone will be on the front or deeper side of an object, and that you're going to get reflex strikes at least two-thirds of the time each day. That means using a sinking lure, such as a worm, jig or tube, that you can drop right into that strike zone.

"Even then, the direction of your presentation can be critical; you have to fish the cover from different angles to see which one is most productive.

"In addition to changing my casting angles, I also work the same cover with different lures," Nixon adds. "The strike zone may be small and in

front of a stump, but if that fish will hit a spinnerbait coming past it, I know I can fish a lot more stumps with that lure than I can with a worm or jig. Different lures also let you work different depths in a variety of ways."

SEASONAL CONSIDERATIONS

Nixon believes bass have the largest strike zone during the prespawn period of spring, which means fast moving lures like spinnerbaits and crankbaits can be among the most productive. Lure presentations do not have to be extremely accurate, because these fish are fairly shallow and usually will chase lures.

However, this changes abruptly when bass begin spawning. Then, they seem to lose nearly all of their aggressiveness. That's when their strike zone is the smallest it will be all year, says Nixon, and that means placing slow falling lures in the center of the strike zone and leaving them there.

The postspawn season generally finds bass in a variety of moods, which means different lure presentations may work, according to Nixon. Aggressive bass that have left nests might prefer faster lures, while nest-guarding bass will want something slow. These conditions change rapidly and are not consistent throughout a lake.

Nixon admits one of his favorite times to fish is during the summer between early June and mid-July, when bass start congregating on structure between 8 and 25 feet deep. And while the strike zone may be large, the specific area used by the fish can be quite small.

"Lure presentation this time of year has to be very precise, and that can be difficult because you're using a depthfinder to find targets," he explains. "I recommend using marker buoys to outline your spot, and start by fishing

Targeted Lures

When the strike zone is small — in summer and winter as well as "tough bite" periods at other times — Nixon relies on precise presentations with targeted lures. Tube lures and finesse worms draw bites when bass are not very active, and the tailspinner is very effective at probing deep bass haunts in winter.

jigs, worms or Carolina rigs to accurately locate the bass. Once you find their location, you might be able to change to a crankbait or even a heavy, deep running spinnerbait."

In the autumn, after the first cold fronts begin cooling the water, Nixon explains, bass move to channel areas such as tributary creeks. The fish usually are shallow, but close to deep water, and sometimes they'll be quite active.

"The strike zone expands considerably during this time of year, and it's a good time to use moving baits like crankbaits, minnows and spinnerbaits," he points out.

The strike zone shrinks again in winter as bass move to deeper water around bluffs, vertical banks and channel bends. Cover loses its importance, and bait becomes the main factor in determining where bass locate.

"If I had to limit myself to one deep water lure for this type of fishing, it would be a lead tailspinner. It provides excellent vibration for such a small lure," Nixon says.

ERRATIC MOVES

At any time of year, Nixon is a firm believer in erratic presentations, such as deflecting a crankbait or spinnerbait off a stump or bouncing a jig over a limb. These sudden changes in direction and vibration, he believes, indicate something abnormal to bass.

"Bass, like all predators, are programmed to attack and eliminate anything that appears weak or abnormal," he says. "When a lure suddenly changes its vibration, a bass reacts."

Thus, while he's initially trying to determine the mood of the fish and how they do want a lure presented, Nixon changes his retrieves on practically every cast.

BIG BASS TACTICS

When the subject changes to big bass, Nixon has these observations on the importance of lure presentation:

"Overall, larger bass have a smaller strike zone,

so you have to be more precise in lure placement, regardless of the season," he says.

"This may not be as hard as it sounds, because I believe big bass relate to objects better. You can sometimes pick out the spot a big bass is most likely to be. It's going to take over the best stump, best brushpile, or the best boat dock around — and every spot will have very easy, fast access to deep water."

Whether you're fishing for big bass or smaller fish, the importance of lure presentation cannot be overemphasized, declares Nixon. Very often, factors as mundane as changing the speed of your retrieve or the angle of your cast can spell the difference between success and failure.

WITH BASS BEING highly pressured in most public fisheries today, fishermen must master a stealthy approach. That means getting into casting position without alerting fish of your presence, and it requires soft, accurate casts. Underhand casts and the flipping and pitching techniques are demanded for soft presentations.

UNTIL YOU KNOW what bass want, you and your buddy should alternate retrieves and presentations until one begins to work. One fisherman can burn a spinnerbait, for example, while the other slow rolls the same lure.

STRIKING MOVES
Hot retrieves for hot action

To FIND BASS, find the baitfish. Everyone knows that rule.

But in summer and fall, finding baitfish doesn't necessarily mean catching bass. Massive schools of baitfish swarm our lakes at those times, driving bass into a feeding frenzy and bass anglers into fits of frustration.

It's especially frustrating to see fish charging through bait schools while ignoring your repeated casts to this surface activity.

CITGO BASSMASTER Tournament Trail pros face this dilemma every autumn and have devised special retrieves that make their lures imitate a baitfish pursued by a bass in a high-speed chase. Pro anglers Jim Morton, Dion Hibdon, Brent Chapman and Danny Correia rely on the following escaping baitfish retrieves to trigger reaction strikes from bass in late summer and throughout fall.

(Opposite page) SINCE BASS are cold-blooded creatures, their metabolisms kick into high gear in warm water. Fast retrieves will trigger vicious strikes.

BASS WILL HIT top-waters throughout the day under overcast skies. For day long action, try working a chugger or popper with a stop-and-go action. You'll find most strikes occur when the lure is sitting still.

HIGH-SPEED CHUGGING

Even though he won the 1992 Oklahoma Invitational in November on a buzzbait, Jim Morton entices bass in autumn by rapidly popping a Storm Lures Rattlin' Chug Bug. The Oklahoma pro developed his escaping baitfish retrieve one fall day when bass were hitting — but not taking — his Chug Bug as it sat still. "It was a frustrating deal until we started working the bait real, real fast and started catching fish," he recalls.

The 3/8-ounce Rattlin' Chug Bug works best for this high-speed retrieve because the lure's size and design allows it to skip and spit water at the same time. Morton also improves the action of his bait by tying a knot directly to the lure, without using a snap or split ring, and pulling the knot snug to the bottom of the line tie. "That keeps the nose of the bait up and causes it to skip a lot quicker," he says.

Keeping his rod at about the 9 o'clock position, Morton jerks the rod and simultaneously reels in line to make the lure pop and skip across the surface. "The faster and the more erratic you can make that bait act while still moving a lot of water and making it spit, the better it's going to be," he says.

If bass ignore his steady retrieve, Morton varies his presentation by popping the lure 4 to 6 feet and then pausing it.

Water Temp And Retrieves

Bass are coldblooded creatures, meaning their body temperature will match that of the water. The colder the water, the slower the fish's metabolism. Consequently, you will want to match lures and retrieves to the water temperature.

Cold water (40 to 60 degrees) — use slow retrieves and compact baits, such as spoons, jigs and grubs.

Moderate temps (60-80 degrees) — speed up your retrieves, using lures that will cover the water quickly. Bass should be feeding actively in this range (except during the spawning ritual). Use spinnerbaits and crankbaits to locate fish, then mop up with worms and other soft plastics once you find them.

Hot water (80 degrees and above) — Bass remain lethargic, sulking in deep cover for long periods between flurries of feeding. Use deep diving crankbaits and Carolina rigs in deep water, but keep an eye out for surface schooling bass, which will hit noisy, fast moving topwaters.

KANSAS PRO Brent Chapman makes his crankbait imitate a fleeing baitfish by bumping the lure into cover — causing it to dart to one side — then reeling quickly to make it swim away from cover.

MATCH LURE ACTION to that of the prevalent forage. A fat body crankbait with a wide wobbling action imitates bluegill and crawfish best, while a slim plug with a tight wiggle matches the swimming action of shad minnows.

"The fast, erratic action excites the bass, and they will follow it," says Morton. "When you stop it and the lure sits there for a minute, bass can't stand it. They'll just explode on the lure."

The constant jerking and reeling can be a tiring ordeal without the proper equipment. Morton recommends using a high-speed reel with a 6.1:1 gear ratio for quickly cranking in slack line and keeping the lure popping. He also uses a 6-foot medium action graphite rod, which is light enough to jerk for hours without wearing him down.

DARTING A JIG

When he wants to induce a strike from inactive bass hanging around docks, Dion Hibdon turns his jig into a fleeing baitfish. The 1997 BASS Masters Classic Champion from Stover, Mo., mimics the action of a scared shad by dropping his jig to the corner of a dock and then quickly reeling it away from his target.

As he approaches a dock or brushpile, Hibdon imagines where the bass is looking, then tries to

place his jig behind the fish and bring it over the top of the bass' head. On the initial fall, Hibdon allows his jig to drop into the shady areas of docks or brushpiles, and then he imparts the escaping baitfish action. "I keep my rod low, and a lot of times I'll make the lure jump with my reel," says Hibdon. With four or five rapid turns of the reel handle, Hibdon can make his jig dart a couple of feet.

Hibdon completes his retrieve by letting the jig fall to the bottom. "A baitfish is not going to run too far away from what it's hiding around — if it gets out there in that open water, it's going to get eaten," says Hibdon, who believes a shad or bluegill darts away from a bass for a short distance then dives into the cover.

The Missouri angler favors a 1/2-ounce jig for this technique because it's heavy enough to stay in the water during the jumping segment of the retrieve and because it falls rapidly for the diving finish. A twin-tail plastic grub trailer gives the lure swimming action.

Since he prefers pitching and skipping his jigs under docks, Hibdon employs a 7-foot medium heavy rod for this technique. "You need a rod that helps you set the hook real fast and that you can control to make good casts," says Hibdon, who works his jigs on 17- to 20-pound-test line.

DEFLECTING CRANKBAITS

During their escape attempts, baitfish tend to accidentally bump into objects, which sometimes leads to their demise, according to Brent Chapman, a former Classic qualifier from Lake Quivera, Kan.

Chapman tries to imitate these bumbling bait-

fish by deflecting a Storm Lures Pro Series Short Wart off stumps, laydowns and pole timber. "When inactive bass are up in shallow water, you can get them to bite by putting something big and loud in front of them," he recommends.

Keeping the tip of his 7-foot rod high, Chapman rapidly retrieves his shallow diving Short Wart. "I've found that faster retrieves are better for getting those reaction strikes," says Chapman. To make his lure more buoyant and help it deflect off cover better, Chapman ties the Short Wart to 20-pound-test line.

A constant high-speed retrieve produces best when Chapman wants to bang the lure into solid wood cover. However, he alters his tactics when presenting the lure around springy cover like cedar trees. Hang-ups occur when running a short-billed crankbait into cedars, so Chapman avoids this problem by cranking his lure at a fast clip to within a few inches of the branches and then stopping it.

"When the bait stops, it sometimes glides in a different direction, almost like it's deflecting off something," says Chapman, who notes that most strikes occur as the lure changes direction.

BURNING SPINNERBAITS

Whenever he finds bass suspending below baitfish on deep, clear lakes, Massachusetts angler Danny Correia burns a spinnerbait across the surface.

This escaping baitfish technique consistently catches smallmouth in northeastern lakes, but he also uses it for largemouth and spotted bass in clear reservoirs throughout the country. He prefers ripping his spinnerbaits along bluffs and deep rocky shoals where the fish suspend as deep as 20 to 30 feet.

A specially designed Fleck spinnerbait is Correia's favorite lure for his high-speed technique. Since he prefers small blades, Correia uses a 1/4-ounce spinnerbait, but adds weight to the lure to make it into a 1/2-ounce model.

"The trouble with most small baits is they don't have enough weight, which causes the lure to pop out of the water when reeled fast. The Fleck spin-nerbait is a small profile bait that I can reel fast without having the bait pop out of the water," says Correia, who swears by a double willowleaf model with a No. 1 and No. 5 blade combination.

Maintaining the right speed is essential to Correia's spinnerbait retrieve. "I try to retrieve it as fast as I possibly can without breaking the water with it," says Correia. Smallmouth ignore his lure if it creates a ripple on the surface, he notes. "But if it's just below the surface and not really waking, they just annihilate it."

If he sees a bass following his spinnerbait, Correia speeds up his retrieve to provoke the fish into striking. He believes bass shy away from the lure if the retrieve is slowed down.

The Massachusetts angler, who placed second in the 1986 Classic, relies on a 7 1/2-foot fiberglass rod and a baitcast reel with a 6.2:1 gear ratio for his spinnerbait technique. He selects 20-pound line because it keeps his spinnerbait near the surface better than lighter monofilament.

The frantic action of a fleeing baitfish drives bass into hot pursuit. Learn to capitalize on this predatory instinct, and you'll have another trick for when bass are picky eaters.

Burning Blades

Smallmouth bass love spinnerbaits with chartreuse blades and skirts — as long as the lures are speeding overhead. Burn all-chartreuse baits through tailwaters where smallies hang out, or in ultraclear water of the upper Midwest and North. To keep the lures from breaking the surface at high speeds and in current, use a heavy model or add extra weight to the lure body.

FLIPPING AND PITCHING
And other underhanded ways to catch bass

THE RUBBER LEGGED,
weedless jig tipped
with a plastic or pork
trailer is the go-to
flipping/pitching bait
for tournament pros.
Jigs attract bigger
bites and are easy to
work into and
through tight spots
where big bass
reside.

FINDING BASS is arguably the first and most difficult step in catching them, but any fisherman unable to deliver the proper presentations will endure some very long days.

Ask any pro angler who has competed in pro-am events to name the main handicap shared by his amateur partners, and he's most likely to mention a lack of "casting consistency."

If you're not satisfied with your ability to hit where you aim, resolve to spend a few hours this spring honing your casting skills. As you do, concentrate on these techniques:

FLIPPING

In its purest form, flipping is used in shallow conditions (generally 5 feet or less) where water depths are more or less consistent. Perhaps the best situation is when bass are located around shallow water targets (dock pilings, reeds, brush, willows, stumps or laydown logs) in a fairly restricted and well-defined depth range.

While it would be nice if these bass holding targets were laid out at a uniform distance from the boat, that doesn't happen in real life. Consequently, much of the success in flipping is

linked to proper boat positioning.

When feasible, veteran flippers prefer a slow, constant trolling motor speed. In these shallow water circumstances, the constant whir of a trolling motor prop is far less disruptive than frequent on/off adjustments.

Although bass fishermen have proved that flipping can be effective in relatively clear water, off-color water is unquestionably the preferred situation for this close-range tactic. Regardless of water clarity, flipping is extremely productive any time bass are positioned close to targets and unwilling to move very far for a meal. Whether it's the result of a passing weather system that drives bass into the center of shallow cover or high-sun conditions that place fish in shaded ambush areas, the result is the same.

While a flipping presentation is more of an underhand swing than anything resembling traditional casting, the object is to deliver a bait on target with a minimum of surface disturbance and a near-vertical fall that lets the bass see the lure before they see the line. Aside from the masking effect of off-color water and thick cover, this is one of the reasons flipping fishermen can generally use heavy line (20- to 30-pound test) without deterring strikes.

To flip, position the boat very close to the target. Point the rod tip up and pull 7 to 8 feet of line off the spool so the lure dangles in front. Lower the rod tip and quickly raise it to start the lure swinging. When it has reached the end of its backward arc, lower the rod with the tip pointed directly at the target, and the jig will swing forward, hitting its mark.

WHEN PRACTICED BY a pro, flipping is a smooth, fluid motion that wastes none of a cast. Experts can hit teacup-size targets 15 feet away, making two or three flips per minute. Little wonder that it's such a deadly technique when bass are scattered in a sea of cover.

AS IN FLIPPING, a pitched lure travels just above the water's surface and lands on target with minimal splash and little noise. Perfection comes from practice and precise spool control.

PITCHING

In what could be termed the long-distance complement to flipping, the pitching technique demands more from an angler in terms of traditional casting skills.

With pitching, an angler can stay away from cover or structure targets and present a lure with the same delicacy one would expect from flipping. Moreover, pitching enables lures to be delivered into areas where a boat can't go and where targets are at varying distances from the boat.

Pitching also employs an underhand motion, but without the limitations of a fixed amount of line. Instead, the reel spool is released and feathered to prevent backlashes and control distance.

Although it stretches even the abilities of professional anglers, effective and accurate pitches can be made at distances of 50 to 60 feet. Standard pitching ranges fall between 15 and 30 feet.

As in flipping, the object of pitching is to present a lure as vertically and as close to the target as possible. This vertical fall is accomplished by casting past the target, drawing the lure on the surface back to the target and then lowering the rod tip to ensure a straight descent. If casting past the target is not practical, an angler can strip line off the reel to create the same vertical presentation.

In any case, the cast itself should be as low and as parallel to the water's surface as possible. By doing so, distance, accuracy and a quiet entry are more consistent and controllable.

While pitching, like flipping, works best when bass are in tight to cover, pitching's applications far exceed those of flipping. It isn't relegated to delivering worms and jigs; the low trajectory and quiet entry can enhance the effectiveness of spinnerbaits, crankbaits and even topwaters. In fact, ac-

complished pitchers often employ pitch casts in all but open water situations.

In becoming proficient at pitching, the right tackle can make a big difference.

Pitching rods generally range from 6 1/2 to 7 1/2 feet long with power ratings similar to flipping sticks, but with lighter tips for casting accuracy and control.

A smooth-working, free-spinning baitcasting reel — balanced to the rod — is crucial in developing one's pitching skills. Equally important is learning how to adjust both magnetic and friction cast controls to get maximum distance with minimum backlash for any-weight lure being used.

With pitching, virtually any line test can be used, depending on the thickness of cover and the weight of the lure (a 1/4-ounce jig might be hard to pitch on 20-pound line).

To pitch, put the reel in free-spool and let out a length of line that is equivalent to the length of the rod. Hold the lure in the free hand so it's even with the reel. Dip the rod tip toward the water and quickly snap it upward while letting go of the lure. The lure should swing forward, traveling on a nearly straight trajectory close to the surface of the water. As the lure moves forward and starts pulling line off the reel, begin lowering the rod tip to control the height the lure travels above the surface. The bait should fall silently and straight down into the target zone. Use the thumb to gently feather the spool as the lure drops.

UNDERHAND CASTING

Forget overhead casting, unless you fish from a seated position. In most fishing situations, the cast you'll want to employ is a simple underhand or slightly sidearm variety.

Trick casting expert Stan Fagerstrom says this most closely resembles the motion used in throwing a softball. However, while the roll of the wrist combined with arm swing creates the momentum, it is the rod tip that transforms this energy into distance and accuracy. Without a fairly limber tip, advises Fagerstrom, it cannot be done effectively.

Pitching Improves Presentation

Joey Monteleone discovered he needed to improve his presentation skills when he grew frustrated with not being able to put his lure close to cover in a river near his home, a spot that was rumored to hold some huge bass.

"Overhanging trees constantly prevented me from casting my bait around the sunken logs and shallow stumps where I knew the bass were hiding," explains the angler and casting expert from Murfreesboro, Tenn. "When I read about pitching in BASS-MASTER, I realized this was the perfect presentation for me."

Pitching, an underhand cast that allows the angler to work a greater distance from his target than flipping, is ideal for getting a lure under overhead obstructions such as tree limbs and boat docks

After practicing in his backyard, Monteleone took his newly learned presentation to the water.

"The results were immediate and astounding," he says.

"And the more I refined my technique, the more and bigger bass I caught — especially bigger."

He often gives novices pointers on pitching at his casting demonstrations.

"The biggest mistakes I see anglers make when learning to pitch are pulling too much line from the reel and pulling too hard on the lure, which loads up the rod tip too much," he says.

"Repetition and consistency are critical to a great presentation," Monteleone adds. "On a 6 1/2-foot rod, I pull out exactly 6 feet, 2 inches of line every time I pitch."

He may change lures, but never lure weights. He usually goes for the smallest artificial lure he can present effectively, since a bass has excellent eyesight and can easily spot the unrealistic properties in a big lure. He routinely pitches a 3/8-ounce jig. When pitching another lure — a worm, spinnerbait, even a Rat-L-Trap — he makes sure it weighs 3/8 ounce as well.

Of critical importance (especially when fishing with a partner) is one's proficiency in both forehand and backhand deliveries. Although backhand casts usually create the most problems for anglers, it is simply the same "softball toss" motion and wrist roll used in forehand presentations. Again, the rod needs to be fairly flexible to accomplish this.

To perform the underhand cast, hold the rod parallel to the water and pointed at the target. Snap the wrist up to begin the cast and allow the rod to "load," or bow backward under the weight of the lure. Without pausing, snap wrist down and allow the rod to load. As the rod tip starts moving upward again, release the line. Still holding the rod parallel to the surface and pointed at the target, snub line when the lure reaches the target.

SKIP CASTING

Instead of settling for bass located close to the edges of docks or overhanging cover, the angler uses a skip cast to put a bait well up under these obstructions — into spots where many bass never see a lure. Like skipping a stone, a lure can be skittered across the surface in the same manner.

Using spinning tackle, the rod is swung low and parallel to the water's surface. Midway through the cast, the rod's motion is stopped abruptly, much like a "checked swing" in baseball. With practice, the timing of the line release with the checked swing becomes second nature. Then, it is a matter of gauging where the bait should hit the water and how far it will skip beyond that im-

pact point. And just like a good skipping stone, smoother, more hydrodynamic lures, such as tube baits, will skip farther and more predictably.

To skip, a right-handed caster should position the boat so his left shoulder is facing the target. Using a golflike sidearm swing, move the rod down and to the side, parallel to the surface of the water, with a very sharp stroke so the lure hits the water in front of the target, then bounces into the desired area. With a little practice, skips of 10 to 15 feet are easy. When using baitcasting gear, practice feathering down the reel spool with the thumb to place the lure precisely and to avoid backlashes.

TO SKIP A LURE beneath a dock, cast low to the water, making the bait bounce across the surface like a flat stone. You can skip with a baitcaster, but the technique is much easier with spinning gear. Some lures work better than others; jigs, grubs and soft jerkbaits can be skipped easily. To skip a Texas rigged soft plastic bait, you'll need to peg the sinker against the hook.

WITH THE weight placed beneath the hook, a drop shot rig lets the lure hover just above the bottom, where it moves and shakes enticingly. Western drop shotters use a small bait hook, which is threaded through the nose of a finesse lure.

FINESSE FISHING: BEYOND THE BASICS
Drop shotting and other lethal tactics

(Opposite page) ALTHOUGH DROP shotting is a finesse presentation, it doesn't mean that you will only catch small bass. Many trophy largemouth have been duped by the small offerings.

I T WAS JULY, and Mark Rizk had not picked up his drop shotting rig since the previous November. But he recognized two things: One, the latest in finesse techniques could work under the highly pressured conditions he was facing, and two, there was no point in playing it safe. After all, this was the 2000 BASS Masters Classic.

Surrounded by other competitors in Lake Calumet, a small 1,000-acre river impoundment connected to Lake Michigan, Rizk made a spirited run at the eventual winner, Woo Daves, falling short by just a little over 1 pound.

On the surface, it would seem foolhardy for the California pro — in this, the most important bass fishing event of his career — to use a technique he had tried only once before. But that is precisely why drop shotting is sweeping through the professional ranks faster than a wind-whipped prairie fire. It *is* that easy, and it *is* that effective.

In its simplest form, drop shotting reverses the normal hook and weight arrangement by placing the sinker below the hook — a hook tied directly to the main line via a Palomar knot. Depending on the situation, the distance between hook and sinker varies from mere inches to several feet.

One Stop Shopping

Drop shotting uses finesse lures, small hooks and light weights suspended beneath the baits. This Don Iovino Drop Shot Kit also includes Top Brass Peg-Its for holding the beads and weights in place.

WHY IT WORKS

"Fishermen need to understand that a high percentage of the fish we catch do not hit a lure out of hunger. They hit our of instinct, reaction or movement. Most of the lures we use for this type of fishing are spinnerbaits, crankbaits and such. However, every bass fisherman in the country knows that the No. 1 artificial lure to catch hungry bass is the plastic worm," says pro Gary Klein.

"For worm fishermen, the slower you can fish the worm, the better. This often boils down to your weight sizes. The lighter the slip sinker, the slower the retrieve. When fish are hungry, that's probably their No. 1 choice. But drop shotting allows an angler to speed things up a bit. With this tactic, a fisherman is actually fishing a rig without any weight. Once that weight hits bottom, the lure becomes a plastic worm with no weight on it. You have the ability to fish it slow and leave it in one place for a long time."

Doodling Does It For Wary Bass

With a flip of his wrist, pro Richard McCarty skips the 5-inch grub to the cover. Anticipating a bite on the bait's slow descent, he concentrates on eliminating any slack in the line.

As the bait drops, he flicks his rod tip, imparting a shivering action to the grub. A bass, suspended along the cover, slowly moves to the bait and inhales the grub. That sends a message to McCarty, who sets the hook with a sweep of the rod. Following a short battle, McCarty brings the 6-pound largemouth to the boat.

It is an impressive show on a highly pressured lake where bass have become extremely wary.

McCarty credits his success to the doodling technique, part of which involves the slow, quivering action he gives the lure. Shaking a finesse bait like that grub often draws bass to investigate and take the bait when nothing else will, says McCarty, a guide on Texas' Lake Fork.

Continuously shaking a Texas rig grub pays off year-round on Lake Fork.

"I don't think the fish see a grub very often," he says. "I use about 2,000 grubs a year. With this technique, I never know whether I'll catch a 2-pounder or a 9-pounder."

Doodling is a technique that transcends time zones. Anytime, anywhere conditions are tough, and in deep water as well as shallow areas — doodling produces.

Whether an angler shakes, swims or simply lets the current move the bait, drop shotting places a lure up in the water column, suspended in a far more natural manner.

THE BASIC DROP SHOT RIG

"Drop shotting is a lot more versatile than I thought," says Rizk. "You can do it in many different depths and around many different types of structure and cover. At the Classic, I caught fish from a 2-foot-deep weedline down to 26 feet on structure."

The one item that stays consistent in every drop shot rig is the Palomar knot used to attach the hook to the line. Care should be taken to bring the final loop down over the hook point to ensure the point faces up, not down, in the water column.

The distance of the line between hook and weight (referred to as the "leader" even though it is still part of the main line) is dependent on the water depth being fished (water clarity generally ranges from clear to slightly stained) and the position of the bass in relation to the bottom.

Identifying the key activity zone with a depthfinder is the best shortcut in determining a

DROP SHOTTING excels when bass are suspended in the tops of deep weeds (left). While the weight hugs the bottom, the lure hovers just above the cover. And when bass are suspended over bare bottoms (right), the height of the lure can be adjusted to the distance above bottom at which bass are holding.

The Palomar Knot

Double the line back through the hook eye to form a loop.
Tie an overhand knot with the doubled line.
Place the loop over the hook, pulling it back to the doubled line as you tighten the knot.
Slowly pull both ends of the line to tighten, making sure the hook is positioned with the point up (as illustrated).

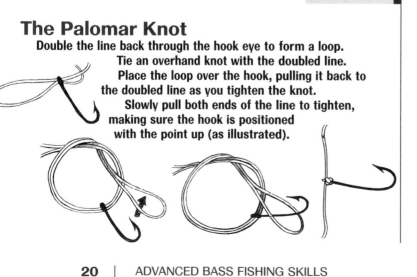

TOP PRO GARY KLEIN, a standout on Western circuits before moving to Texas, quickly saw the value of adding drop shotting to his repertoire of bass techniques. In many ways, he says, drop shotting outperforms Carolina rigging.

Traditional Doodling

Don Iovino, known as the father of doodling, defines the technique as shaking a finesse bait, 4 to 6 inches in length, with a brass weight and glass bead. When the angler shakes or "doodles" the bait, mainly on the fall, it shivers and slides, tempting wary bass to strike.

The shaking action of the bait is accomplished by manipulating the rod tip with the wrist, similar to the rhythmic rapping of a pencil on a desk top. The brass and glass produce a clacking noise that attracts bass. Many believe the sound mimics that of a crawfish.

The water depth determines the amount of weight. Iovino recommends a 1/8-ounce sinker for water from 1 to 15 feet deep, a 5/32-ounce sinker for 15 to 25 feet and a 3/16-ounce weight for deeper than 25 feet. Iovino suggests that anglers use a fire-polished, faceted glass bead.

Traditionally, doodling is a vertical presentation of a hand-poured worm to bass that are suspended over a deep breakline or along bluffs and cliffs. This same vertical approach is effective on bass suspended in standing timber, over brushpiles, along bridge pilings or beneath boat docks. When bass are suspended alongside structure or cover, doodling a grub slowly through the strike zone will often outproduce a faster falling, larger profile jig.

starting point for leader length. While Japanese anglers often use very short, 4- to 5-inch leaders, California pro Aaron Martens normally keeps the distance somewhere in the 6- to 10-inch range.

In drop shotting, sinker weights normally range from 1/16 ounce to as much as 3/8 ounce. And when it comes to sinker types, the choices can vary from the most basic and pedestrian bell sinker to ultraexpensive tungsten weights equipped with swiveling line clips.

Depending on the application, cover and structure present, line tests also span a fairly wide spectrum, with the basic rig sporting 8- to 10-pound test. Tackle choices are similarly broad, with spinning tackle being the best choice for deep water or light weights, while baitcasting gear is better-suited to higher line tests, thicker cover and shallow water conditions.

At the business end of things, a bass angler needs two basic types of hooks: (1) a short-shank, bait-holder style in No. 2 and No. 4 sizes used for nose-hooking baits where cover is sparse, and (2) a wide gap worm hook in a size appropriate (typically 1/0 or 2/0) for the length and thickness of the lure being fished.

WHEN AND WHERE TO WORK IT

In the hands of a creative fisherman, a drop shot rig can work any time of year. For the beginning drop shotter, however, a good starting point in learning the technique is summer through fall.

In summer, bass in impoundments often position themselves over deeper structure, near channel edges or breaklines. While jigs, Texas rig plastics and Carolina rigs can produce strikes in these situations, an angler is forcing the fish to move and react to the bait. With a drop shot rig, the lure can be placed directly in front of them — and kept there almost indefinitely.

The Drop Shot Rig

Components for a drop shot rig include a special round weight with a quick clip system, a small hook and tiny drop shot lure, such as this minnow. To attach the weight, slide the end of the line through the clip and pull it firmly into the V of the wire.

Sight Fishing

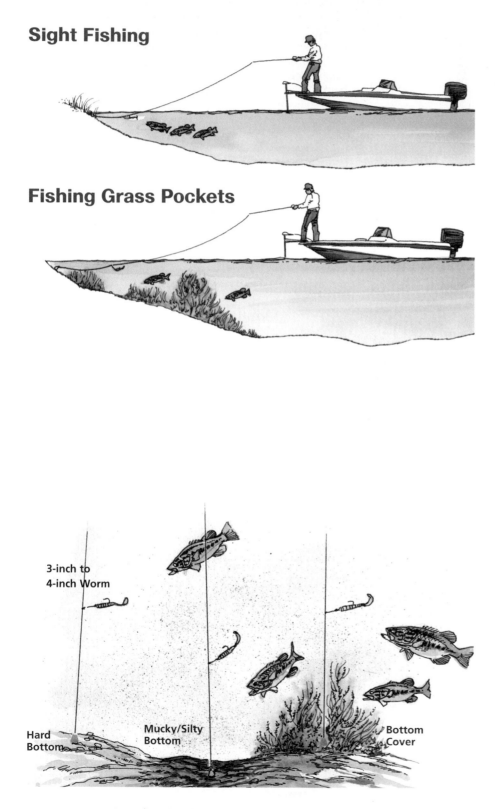

Fishing Grass Pockets

3-inch to
4-inch Worm

Hard
Bottom

Mucky/Silty
Bottom

Bottom
Cover

HORIZONTAL DROP SHOTTING
(Top) When bass are spawning or cruising in shallow water, cast a drop shot rig to your target and drag it carefully until the lure — but not the weight — is in the strike zone. Shake the line until a fish strikes.
(Bottom) Fish grass pockets with a drop shot rig in much the same manner. While the weight is hidden in weeds, the lure hovers in place in openings within the weedbeds.

Klein's No. 1 drop shotting scenario is during autumn, when the lake levels are low and thermoclines have disappeared. With bass focusing on shad and relating to channel edges, dropoffs and bottom contour changes, Klein looks for the most ideal situation he can find, such as a bluff bank cutting across a flat with deep water access nearby.

However, it would be a mistake to categorize drop shotting as merely a vertically oriented/offshore/deeper water tactic. Already, many pro anglers have discovered its shallow water potential.

A drop shot rig makes a perfect sight fishing tool. Cast it ahead of cruising, prespawn fish, or drop it directly onto a bed. In the latter situation, the weight should be cast beyond the bed — on dry land, if necessary — then slowly pulled back until the lure is positioned directly above the bedding area. By lowering and then lifting the rod tip, a fisherman can make repeated presentations over a bass' "hot zone" without making repeated casts.

This "horizontal" drop shotting tactic also can be employed in grassbed pockets. Again, the weight is cast beyond the open

A DROP SHOT RIG keeps the bait above problem bottoms, such as muck, silt and cover. A Texas or Carolina rigged lure might quickly become fouled in such situations, but a drop shot lure remains above the slop.

water and retrieved until the lure can be slowly lowered directly into the pocket. Unlike traditional methods, in which the bass is forced to react to a lure that briefly trespasses through its domain, a drop shot bait can be kept there until a fish responds.

CALIFORNIA'S DON IOVINO is one of the foremost authorities on finesse tactics, including drop shotting, split shotting and doodling. This big spotted bass is proof that you don't always have to use spinning gear to enjoy success with finesse.

HOW THE PROS WORK IT

Mark Rizk — Whenever possible, he nose-hooks hand-poured plastic baits with a No. 4 Gamakatsu G-Loc hook positioned anywhere from 12 inches to 5 feet above the weight. Below the hook, he slides on a 1/4-ounce brass slip sinker and ties a split ring at the end of the line to stop the weight. To create a clicking sound, he sometimes adds a glass bead between the split ring and the sinker.

"Most of the time, I'm shaking the bait. But I don't shake the weight — I leave a big loop in my line above the water and shake that big loop," says Rizk. "Most of the time, there is no indication of a strike; it's just a pressure bite. I'll shake that loose loop, lift the rod and feel for pressure. When I get pressure, it's generally a fish."

Gary Klein — As a general rule, Klein will increase leader length with water depth and correspondingly upgrade sinker weights; that is, he uses 1/16- to 1/8-ounce sizes in shallow water and 3/16- or 1/4-ounce weights in deeper water.

His standard spinning rig setup centers around a 6-6 medium light rod and spinning reel spooled with 6- or 8-pound-test fluorocarbon line.

"Drop shotting is a lot like fishing a jigging spoon, because you're going around finding fish on your depthfinder. The way a drop shot bait swims, probably 30 percent of your hits will come on the initial drop; if the bait goes directly through the fish, it will never hit bottom."

Doodling Tackle

The traditional doodling rod is a 6 1/2-foot, medium action graphite spinning rod with a sensitive tip. A medium/heavy butt is required for a good hook set, and a sensitive tip is necessary to detect the "pressure bites." Doodling anglers prefer 6 1/2- to 7-foot rods for deep water, because the longer rods move more line on the hook set.

Setting the hook with light monofilament line at extreme depths can be very difficult, pro Jay Yelas says.

"If you're fishing water 30 feet or deeper, and you simply set the hook the normal way, you're not really doing much more than stretching the line," he notes. "If I feel I have a bite, I collect any slack prior to setting the hook. I get the rod bent and keep it bent throughout the battle. As the fish is brought back to the boat, the struggle will work the hook in deeper."

If hook set continues to be a problem, then it's reasonable to assume that the hook could be the culprit. Yelas recommends a strong, light wire hook with an extremely sharp point for maximum penetration.

Through the years, bass fishermen have shown themselves to be very innovative, taking an excellent idea like doodling and applying it to their special regional situations. Those fishing the heavily pressured lakes of northeast Texas are finding that a 3- or 5-inch grub doodled in and around brush and timber, draws strikes from bass that will not hit larger plastics or jigs. In addition, many anglers now doodle Reapers, paddle-tail grubs and 6-inch doodle worms.

With a little imagination, you can adapt these finesse techniques to your own tough-bite conditions, whether they occur in deep or shallow water. Expand your repertoire while increasing your bassin' success — give doodling a try.

CAROLINA RIGGING
An easy and effective way to seine the water

WHETHER YOU'RE fishing sparse grass, rocks or stumps in shallow water, or structure in deep water, Carolina rigging puts your lure in front of more bass in a shorter period of time.

SOME BASS FISHING TECHNIQUES are a bear to master, but not Carolina rigging. Like most great ideas, the genius of this lure presentation method lies in its simplicity. First introduced to the national bass fishing audience two decades ago, Carolina rigging has be-come a mainstay of tournament pros, weekend bass club competitors and beginning anglers alike.

In fact, Carolina rigging is now easily the No. 1 method for fishing a soft plastic lure. Once re-garded strictly as a warmwater technique, a grow-ing number of anglers rely on the rig year-round.

Carolina Components

Prerigged Carolina rigs (top left) are quicker and easier to replace should your line break. To make your own, you'll need a sinker, a glass bead, a barrel swivel, a wide gap hook and a soft plastic lure of your choice.

GOLD STANDARD

"There probably are more bass caught on Carolina rigs today than by any other method," notes Tennessee bass guide Jack Christian. "A decade ago, only tournament anglers who were up on the latest techniques were using it, but now it's the gold standard for fishing soft plastics."

The guide believes that with a little practice, anyone can catch bass on a Carolina rig from the first day he or she tries it.

"It's so much easier for inexperienced clients to cast, retrieve and catch fish with a Carolina rig than with a Texas rig. The heavy sinker is a breeze to cast long distances. I just tighten the cast control knob on my baitcasting reels, and even a client who's never used a baitcaster before can sling it a country mile without backlashing. You get a ton of bites with the system, too, which makes for a more exciting and enjoyable outing."

Long typecast as a keeper-bass method, Carolina rigging is producing more lunker bass for anglers with the savvy to modify it for big fish.

"For years, the accepted purpose of a Carolina rig was to catch a quick limit. After that, you'd switch to a spinnerbait or jig for bigger fish," Christian notes. "But once anglers began experimenting with larger lures, they started catching bigger bass on it. If I'm on a lake known for big fish, I may fish a 9-inch lizard or an 11-inch worm on it. I know trophy hunters in Texas and Florida who use 16-inch worms on Carolina rigs." "You'll catch a lot more big bass under adverse weather conditions with a Carolina rig than with a Texas rig," pro Charlie Ingram adds. "It's much easier to cast into the wind, and it's more effective on deep

Some Carolina riggers prefer to drag the setup along the bottom, moving it just inches at a time with a sideways sweep of the rod. Pause between drags.

Others like to hop the rig by raising the rod tip, reeling up slack between lifts. Where the bottom is littered with rocks or brush, you'll hang up less by lifting the rod vertically.

structure. But most important, you can fish it slower. You only have to pull the sinker across the bottom a few inches at a time to activate the worm or lizard on the end of the leader, and coax a sluggish bass into biting."

COMPONENTS OF SUCCESS

Both Christian and Ingram have spent considerable time fine-tuning the various components of their Carolina rigs to produce more bites. They offer the following to Bassmasters hoping to enhance their productivity with the rig:

Tackle — "Use gear that allows you to cast the rig long distances, retrieve it slowly and detect light bites quickly," Christian advises. The guide fishes his Carolina rigs on a medium heavy 6-foot, 8-inch baitcasting rod. "I've tried longer rods, but they're tiring to fish with all day," he says. Christian mates the rod with a reel that has a moderate retrieve speed. "Stay away from those high-speed reels when Carolina rigging," he advises. The guide spools up with small diameter P-Line, 25-pound test for his main line and 12 for his leaders.

Unlike most anglers, Ingram often fishes Carolina rigs on spinning gear. "I can feel the lure much better on spinning gear, and this is definitely a situation where feel is 90 percent of the game. Remember, you've got a big sinker and 2 feet or more of leader between your main line and the hook to dampen the sensation of a bite. You don't get that familiar 'tap' when a bass strikes like you do when Texas rigging." Ingram's main stick for Carolina rigging is a stiff action 6 1/2-foot spinning rod. He spools up with 30-pound test for his main line and 12 pound for his leader.

Sinkers — "One of the biggest mistakes I see anglers make with a Carolina rig is using a sinker that's too light," Ingram says. "The whole point of the system is to get the sinker to the bottom quickly and keep it there." Both men favor 3/4-ounce sinkers, but don't hesitate to go to 1 ounce in deep water or high winds.

Hooks — "Since you want the lure to have a buoyant, lifelike action behind the sinker, it's imperative to use a lightweight hook," Christian says. "On most lures, I use a 4/0 Gamakatsu Extra Wide Gap worm hook; the oversized gap lets the hook point clear the ball of wadded-up plastic that forms when a bass inhales your lure."

"I like small hooks on my Carolina rigs," Ingram counters. "They're easier to stick in light-biting bass and harder for 'em to shake." The pro prefers Mustad MegaBite hooks in 1/0 or 2/0 for all but his biggest lures.

SEASON AFTER SEASON

Ingram and Christian offer these seasonal tips for scoring more strikes on Carolina rigs:

Prespawn — "In cold water, target staging areas you'd normally fish with a suspending jerkbait, such as the first dropoff adjacent to a slow-tapering point or spawning flat," Christian advises. "Also use the rig to probe migration routes,

including ditches and creek channels. Try a small lure like a 4-inch lizard or grub rigged on an extra-long leader, up to 48 inches; this gives a sluggish bass plenty of freedom of movement so it has time to suck in the lure completely without detecting the sinker and rejecting the bait."

Spawn — "Don't underestimate the power of a Carolina rig to catch bedding bass," Ingram says. "It's especially deadly in lakes where bass spawn on shallow offshore bars and humps. Of course, a lizard is the classic spawning bass lure, but try a big tube bait like Lunker City's Toob as well. Fish the rig superslow for bedding bass. If you feel the sinker strike an object like a stickup or stump, stop and shake the rod tip gently to activate the lure. Set the hook immediately when you detect any resistance."

Postspawn — "The rig really comes into its own now as bass scatter out across big pieces of structure," Christian says. "Many bassers turn to a crankbait now, but a slow moving Carolina presentation will outfish crankbaits 3 to 1 on days when bass aren't especially active. For a big bass, try a less active lure like a 6-inch straight-tail worm, or a shad mimic like a French Fry, tube jig or 5-inch grub. Target the tips of long points, the sides of humps and other open water structure with a deep access close by."

Summer — "Fish deeper — creek channel drops, main lake bars and offshore ledges will all hold bass," Ingram says. "Instead of working the rig down a drop, try fishing it parallel to the structure, targeting first the top and then the deeper stages of the descent. Try a soft jerkbait. In grass, use a leader that's long enough to allow the bait to suspend above the vegetation, then bulk up your lure — a 10-inch worm can be awesome in weedy lakes. Use rattle inserts in your baits and metal clackers on your rig to create more noise."

Fall — "The lake is often at its clearest now, so consider using smaller lures like French Fries in realistic baitfish colors on a lighter leader," Christian notes. "This is also a good time to try a hard bait like a floating minnow lure on a Carolina rig; these work great in rocky highland reservoirs around deep points."

WANT BIGGER BASS on your Carolina rig? Use a bigger lure, advises Charlie Ingram, who often uses a 9-inch lizard in warm water.

Winter — Ingram doesn't do much Carolina rigging in frigid water, but Christian does, for smallmouth, especially. "I've caught big smallies in 38 degree water on Carolina rig lizards fished on the edge of the river channel in the 20-foot zone," he says. "You've got to barely move the sinker to get bit, and a lure with a lot of salt, like a Gene Larew lizard, really helps. Bass that bite lightly seem to hold on to it longer. And don't think all lunker smallmouth are sluggish in cold water — I've had 'em rip the rod right out of my hands!"

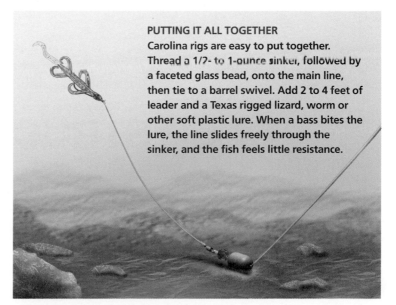

PUTTING IT ALL TOGETHER
Carolina rigs are easy to put together. Thread a 1/2- to 1-ounce sinker, followed by a faceted glass bead, onto the main line, then tie to a barrel swivel. Add 2 to 4 feet of leader and a Texas rigged lizard, worm or other soft plastic lure. When a bass bites the lure, the line slides freely through the sinker, and the fish feels little resistance.

DEEP STRUCTURE PRIMER

When the going gets tough, the tough go deep

IT IS A WHOLE NEW WORLD TO MOST bass enthusiasts, fishing's version of Sea Quest. Offshore, deep water structure represents the final frontier for many anglers. Yet, with the exception of the spring spawn, many bass spend their entire lives in an environment where depth provides a layer of security. And when it comes to deep structure fishing, most fishermen are in the dark.

That is even true in the professional ranks, where the most successful competitors are those who have taken the time to perfect techniques for locating and dissecting bass-holding structure that

And in the process, their words and experiences lessen the mysterious nature of the deep water bass lair.

DAVID FRITTS: CHANNELS AND LEDGES

Former B.A.S.S. Angler of the Year and BASS Masters Classic champion David Fritts is probably the most recognizable deep water specialist in America. Best known as a cranking expert, the North Carolina pro is partial to reservoir fishing, particularly the channels and ledges formed along rivers and creeks.

"Ledges and channels are places I fish a lot throughout the year," Fritts says. "They are probably the most productive areas to fish a crankbait, because they offer so many different types of structure: rocks or stumps or even brush."

That is Lesson 1. Fritts targets only the sections of a channel edge or ledge that have some secondary form of cover (rock or wood). Lesson 2: Concentrate on the bends in the channel.

"I shy away from the big bends that everybody sees on a map," he explains. "And I like to fish the inside bends instead of the outside bends. I look for structure that is not very obvious."

Pick Your Poison
Fishing for deep water bass is not rocket science, but lure selection is critical. Spoons, blade baits and superheavy spinnerbaits will get anglers in the strike zone faster, and keep the baits in front of bass for longer periods of time.

is too deep to be seen. These men learned long ago that such offshore structure harbors the least pressured bass and, some would claim, the most reliable fishing.

They have paid their dues, mastered the craft of deep structure fishing and have plenty of lessons to share. Individually, our experts discuss the aspects of locating and catching deep bass, their favorite offshore haunts and the tools they use to mine these areas. Collectively, they provide a crash course in probing deep structure.

Go With
The Flow

The proper way to retrieve a crankbait through bass cover along a channel is with the current, David Fritts believes.

MARK DAVIS: HIS ELECTRONIC EYES

"Liquid crystal technology has made me a lot better fisherman, without a doubt," Mark Davis says. "In the Classic on High Rock (Lake), I relied on my electronics for two things: I was able to pinpoint baitfish, and I was able to almost exactly position the bass that were suspended in relation to the brush and the bottom.

"My electronics gave me the confidence to stay on certain brushpiles, and I was able to catch fish because of it. I just stayed around them and kept trying different angles and different presentations until I triggered a fish into biting."

Davis' Classic-winning pattern involved fishing several towering brushpiles positioned in 15 to 16 feet of water. The bass moved up and down the water column throughout the day, and most were caught at 6 to 8 feet off the bottom.

By understanding the depth of the bass and baitfish, Davis concentrated on adjusting the position of his rod tip to keep his spinnerbait and crankbait traveling at the proper level. Bringing the lure past the fish at the same depth was a key to getting strikes.

Lesson 3 involves the proper boat positioning to saturate a potentially good stretch of a channel or ledge. Fritts will parallel the edge during the times when most of the bass are positioned out along the breakline. But his Ranger boat can usually be found sitting out over deep water and pointed toward the shallower side. This positioning allows his crankbait to dig up the bottom of the ledge before dropping off into deep water — a combination that bass apparently find hard to resist.

Many times, a channel/ledge situation involves fishing current. Over the years, Fritts has learned to appreciate this constant flow, which can position bass predictably and make them more aggressive.

"Current dictates how the fish are going to be positioned on certain types of structure, which is a real advantage that you don't have with most deep water situations," he says. "Once you figure out that positioning, you simply go to similar spots along the channel, and you'll find the bass in the same position on the same spot along the structure."

Initially, Fritts retrieves his crankbait with the current. He also will crank "cross-current" along the ledge. He rarely bothers with cranking against the current, which is not the natural direction bass expect food to wash by.

Underwater
Eyes

Mark Davis uses his bow depthfinder to spot brushpiles and any baitfish and bass nearby.

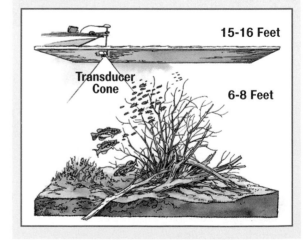

15-16 Feet

Transducer
Cone

6-8 Feet

"I was really able to dissect the cover, see the bass and make the right presentation," he adds. "Those fish weren't spooky and two or three times I actually went over the brush real slow with my trolling motor. One time, I saw a 3-pounder next to a ball of shad and I immediately turned and made a cast right directly behind the boat and cranked the lure down. The fish hit no more than 10 feet behind the prop.

"I would have never made that cast had I not seen the fish on my electronics."

Quality depthfinding electronics enabled him to perform surgery on the brushpiles and its resident bass. It was a lesson that wasn't lost on Mark Davis.

TODD FULK: ROADBED HOT SPOTS

Roads and highways submerged during the flooding of a reservoir are among the most universal of bass structures. That's one reason why they may be Todd Fulk's favorite places to fish. Another is that roadbeds are not the easiest structures to fish, so they harbor relatively unpressured schools of bass.

"I love finding and fishing roadbeds, but not just any old roadbed," says Fulk, a North Carolina pro and past Classic qualifier. "I don't waste my time on a straight road. If it has a bend in it or any irregular features along it, then I get excited."

On lakes in his home state — especially High Rock and Kerr (Buggs Island) — Fulk developed a talent for exploiting roadbeds. He especially has a knack for finding hot spots where bass usually congregate along the otherwise straight and smooth roadways.

Fulk searches for bends and curves, adjacent weedlines, rocky foundations, bridges (his absolute favorite), intersections with a channel or another road, roadside ditches and culverts, and nearby fencerows.

In winter, Fulk targets these unusual features with a 3/4-ounce Hopkins spoon. This is usually a time when the bass will be suspended just off roadbeds, and vertical jigging

is the best method of presenting a lure to them. The rest of the year, his two most productive offerings are a deep diving crankbait and a Carolina rig.

His approach involves first covering the secondary structure with a Poe's 400 Series crankbait in search of the most active bass. He then sweeps the spot with a Carolina rig lizard, which has long been his most productive tool for working roadbeds.

His Carolina setup consists of a 6-inch watermelon- or pumpkinseed-colored lizard, 3/0 offset hook, 3-foot leader of 10- to 17-pound-test line (depending on water clarity) and 3/4-ounce weight. When bass are especially inactive, Fulk switches to a 3-inch white grub on a 1/0 hook.

"The key with the lizard is to make long casts," Fulk says. "After dropping a marker buoy near the spot I want to fish, I throw well beyond the buoy and drag the lizard back to that spot. That approach seems to be less threatening and more effective that just dropping the Carolina rig down right on the spot."

A Road Less Traveled

Todd Fulk believes roadbeds offer a variety of potential hideouts for bass, including many that are rarely fished.

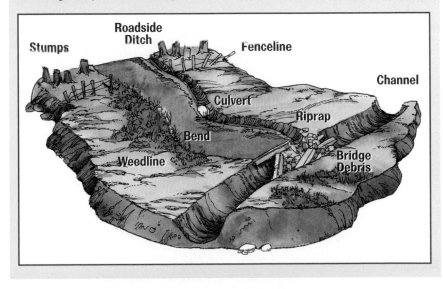

Angles Of Attack

Robert Hamilton has learned to try several retrieve angles (top illustration) to find the one most likely to draw a strike. To get a reaction bite, he tries to bump the cover with his crankbait (bottom illustration).

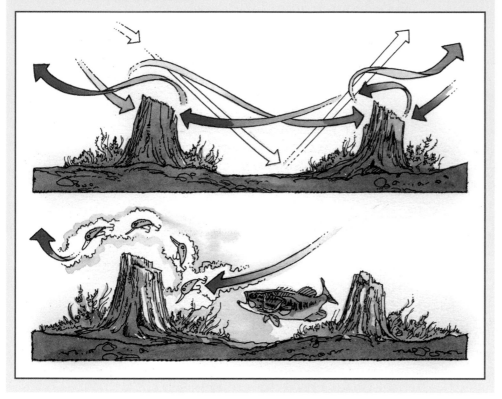

of structure. I always fish two or three different angles with several different lures. And with structure like humps, you want to circle it and fish it from every angle with each bait. There is usually a certain angle that deep structure fish will bite from.

"The '92 Classic was a prime example. A lot of the places I fished had been fished by other guys. But they were fishing them from other angles and not catching bass. Depending on the wind or the current or whatever, certain areas on a piece of structure will produce strikes, once you figure out the angle to bring the lure. And this will hold true day in and day out on that structure."

Hamilton believes anglers significantly limit themselves with a single lure and retrieve angle because a bass on that structure may simply be positioned away from the path of the bait. Changing angles and lures enables him to work the area thoroughly, and even catch bass that are roaming and not facing in any one direction.

ROBERT HAMILTON: ANGLES AND COVERAGE

In July 1992, the fishing world discovered what his fellow competitors had already known about Robert Hamilton: that he is an outstanding deep structure fisherman. Hamilton won the 1992 Classic on Alabama's Lake Logan Martin on the strength of a deep water pattern that involved several different lures.

Over the years, the Mississippi pro has developed some interesting — and productive — theories about lure presentations to offshore-structure bass.

"You can fish over top of a lot of fish with deep structure. The key is never fish one bait on a piece

"Another misleading thing about deep water fishing, especially with a crankbait or spinnerbait, is that people don't think about getting a reaction-type strike like you would if you were bringing those lures past a shallow stump," Hamilton continues. "Most people think of an impulse/reaction bite as being a shallow water situation.

"It's not limited to shallow water. If a fish is dormant and resting beside a stump in deep water, you can bring a worm or jig by and never get a reaction. But if you bump a crankbait into that stump or crash a spinnerbait through a deep water brushpile, you're likely to get a reactionary bite. Deflection is a key, even in deep water."

ADDING WEIGHT to a crankbait has several benefits for anglers keying on deep bass: It allows anglers to make longer casts, giving the bait an opportunity to dive deeper; and it makes buoyant crankbaits suspend in the strike zone.

DAVID ASHCRAFT: THE MOST OVER-LOOKED STRUCTURE

From his days as an emerging fisherman in the natural lakes and artificial reservoirs of Arkansas, David Ashcraft has grown capable of seining the resident bass off any type of deep structure — his favorite type of fishing.

But there is one particular deep water situation that he seeks out on reservoirs throughout the South, and it usually becomes his private domain. It may be the most subtle and overlooked type of structure of all.

"One of the things I like to find is where an old grinding mill was once built out near a creek channel," says Ashcraft, who utilized his deep water skills to qualify for the 1995 Classic. "A lot of river and creek systems used to have the old grinding mills. That's how everybody got their meal and flour in the old days.

"These are not community fishing holes, by any means. You won't find them on a map. Some have been silted in, and it takes a lot of work and looking with your electronics to find places like this. But once you do, it can be a gold mine."

The residue from these mills is attractive to bass for a variety of reasons. First, the mills are traditionally built on a flat area adjacent to a deep running creek. On the other side of the old mill site will be a smooth bottom that once served as a road for horse-drawn wagons and the first motorized vehicles. Remnants of the mill's rocky foundation and other debris often remain.

But the most attractive portion is the deep hole that was created by the constant flood of water that came off the paddle wheel that pow-

ered the mill's grinder. This hole, usually 20 to 25 feet in diameter, is often 8 to 18 feet deeper than the surrounding terrain, according to Ashcraft.

"This hole is an excellent place for bass to move up and down, so it is *the* hot spot," he praises. "The bass will go into that hole and suspend when they're inactive. Then they'll move right up onto the flat or the old foundation to feed."

Ashcraft uses his electronics to determine whether the fish are suspended or up on the edge of the flat.

"I'll first throw a big (Tennessee shad or fire-tiger Storm) Wiggle Wart and crank the whole mill area. Once the bass convince me that they're not going to bite the crankbait, my next choice is a 1-ounce spinnerbait, which I throw up onto the flat and slow roll back down into the hole and let it drop. Finally, I'll go to a Carolina rig.

"These old mills always hold fish."

David Ashcraft's private sanctuaries are just one example of the value of deep structure fishing. It is a payoff rarely found with shallow water angling.

Milling Around

They aren't depicted on contour maps, but if you can find the submerged site of an old mill along a creek, you should load up on bass, says David Ashcraft.

ADVANCED BASS FISHING SKILLS

LURES

Baits are a bass angler's tools;
each is made for specific tasks . . .

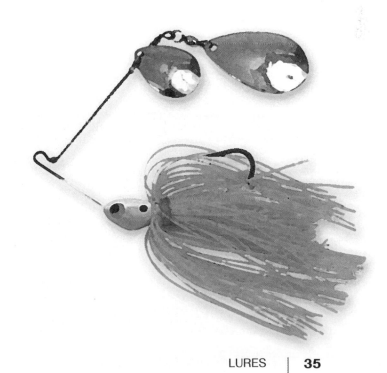

PROS KNOW that subtle changes in the appearance of baits can result in a substantial increase in bites. If bass are biting spinnerbaits, fine-tune your offering by trying different blade sizes, types and colors to get the most out of the pattern.

(Opposite page) A MASTER at the guessing game, Rick Clunn has won 14 B.A.S.S. tournaments by allowing intuition and experience to guide his lure selection.

HOW THE PROS KNOW WHAT TO THROW

There's more to choosing lures than luck

A S A KID, the bass angler was a puzzle freak. He loved jigsaws. He'd pick up the odd-shaped cuts of cardboard and twirl them around to see if they'd fit. He thrived on the challenge and thrilled with accomplishment when he pushed the last piece into place.

Today, as an adult, he faces a different sort of puzzle. And this one is yielding frustration instead of fun. He's fished for four hours without getting a bite. He's tried bait after bait, and nothing has worked. Now he's fumbling through two open tackleboxes, a sack of plastic worms and a box of odds-and-ends lures, trying to decide what to throw next.

This angler's perplexity is shared by his comrades-at-rods wherever line meets water. Today's bait choice is so large and diverse that it boggles many Bassmasters' minds. Consider the options: lure size, color, action, feel, sound, smell, taste; depth at which various lures may be fished; speed with which they may be fished. Some lures resemble natural prey; others don't. Some can be fished through heavy cover; others snag on a spider web.

No wonder there's so much confusion! Like our puzzle solver above, most fishermen own hundreds of lures from which they must choose the exact one to catch bass under their given set of circumstances.

This is where the pros can help. Fish-for-pay anglers have to be good at selecting the right lures, or they won't be on the tournament circuit long. Tour regulars travel the country and continuously fish diverse waters and conditions. Each day calls for new lure decisions, and he who decides best wins the most. In the process, these anglers quickly gain experience in terms of knowing what to throw.

Average anglers can borrow from the pros' expertise and shortcut their way to better lure selection. Here is what two of the best have to say:

SIZE MATTERS

When soft plastics are the go-to bait, choosing the right size can be the difference between a full livewell and being skunked. Here are some things to consider before making a decision:

■ Just because bass aren't biting your 6-inch worm, don't think they want something smaller. Sometimes the presentation is the problem. Remember that bigger worms sink slower, and bass respond favorably to this action.

■ Bass are lazy, especially in frigid weather. Big largemouth want more bang for their bucks, and will eat a 12-inch worm over a 4-inch worm simply because the meal offers more nutrition for the energy expended.

■ Match the hatch. Know the size of the main forage base of the lake you are fishing, and duplicate this profile with your plastic offerings.

■ If all else fails, go little. Big baits can offend wary bass. Finesse worms may be small, but they can generate big bites.

WHEN FISHING CUR-
RENT, Jay Yelas uses
heavy baits that will
resist being con-
trolled by fast flow-
ing water. Yelas also
emphasizes working
lures downcurrent, as
reeling a bait upcur-
rent is unnatural and
will not elicit many
strikes.

BE VERSATILE AND SYSTEMATIC

Woo Daves of Virginia is known as "Mr. Top Five" because of his history of high finishes in the BASS Masters Classic.

"I think I won in Illinois because I picked the best bait," he reveals of his first place finish in the 1991 Illinois BASSMASTER Invitational. "I threw an 8-inch worm when other fishermen around me were throwing smaller worms. My bigger worm took longer to fall, and the bass liked this slower presentation."

How did Daves know to try the bigger worm? "Experience," he explains matter-of-factly. "I learned a long time ago that picky bass — and these were — prefer a slower falling bait over one that falls fast."

Weekend anglers don't have this wealth of experience on which to bank, but Daves says there's another, simple way to get a line on the right lure — literally. "They can check at the local bait shop. I do this every time I go to a new lake, and I can usually pick up some reliable information about

what baits and colors the fish are hitting best.

"Some lures or colors work in one region but not in others. I've seen this many times. For instance, bright red is a good worm color in Texas, but I haven't had much luck with it in other areas. The point is, you can learn these local favorites by asking. And they're favorites for a reason. They catch fish on that particular body of water."

Still, this is only the beginning of the lure selection process, and Daves doesn't rely solely on this advice. Besides the local favorite, he also tries several other baits. After considering such variables as time of year, water and weather conditions, natural prey and dominant structure, he comes up with a short list of lures for trial-and-error testing.

"I usually try a worm, a crankbait and a spinnerbait. I alternate using these lures or others I think might be good. Then when I come to an unusual piece of structure, a spot I think should really hold some fish, I'll try everything I've got tied on. This way I let the bass tell me which lure they want."

The Woo System Of Lure Selection

This is Daves' overall approach to lure selection:

1. "When the water's clear, I stick with light colors — white, chrome, pearl. In worm fishing, I use a worm that I can see light coming through. In stained water, I switch to darker colors like chartreuse or yellow. And in muddy water, I go to the brightest or darkest colors; orange, brown, black."

2. "I use smaller baits in lakes and rivers where there are a lot of little bass but not many big ones. But in lakes with a good number of big fish, I use small baits in early spring, and then I upgrade in size in late spring and summer. When the water starts cooling down in fall, I go back small again."

3. "When bass are active — I can see them chasing baitfish, or they're striking hard — I fish faster baits like crankbaits, spinnerbaits and buzzbaits. But when they're tight to cover and not chasing, I switch to worms and jigs."

4. "One thing I'm trying more and having success with is big spinnerbaits and worms in clear water. This goes against what most people have been saying over the years, but it's working."

5. "It's best to stick with just a few basic baits. Most weekend anglers have too many different baits. I think it's better to have several of the same type and color baits that have different lips to cover different depths of water, or in spinnerbaits, different-size bodies and blades."

WOO DAVES recommends that weekend anglers focus on only a handful of baits that they have confidence in, but keep several sizes and colors handy.

Daves adds that his selections vary from one lake and one time to the next. For instance, he may substitute a jig for the worm or a topwater for the spinnerbait if these are logical choices on a given day. Still, he steadfastly casts a menu of baits until he detects a preference for one. (He does this during tournament practice. Ideally, he has narrowed his choice to one or two baits by the first day of competition.)

"Now, this is important," he emphasizes. "After you catch your first fish, stop and analyze the spot, the lure, the presentation, how the bass bit. This is the best way to figure out the right lure. Just use some trial-and-error testing with the most logical baits until you see a preference for one of them. You have to pay attention to what the fish tell you."

Daves feels the biggest mistake average anglers make in lure selection is not deciphering the subtle hints the fish give. "Pay attention, and repeat whatever brings you success. Then, once you're in the ballpark, you can make subtle changes that are necessary. You can put on different blades, pick another bait size; whatever you need to do."

CONFIDENCE LURES

Ron Shuffield of Arkansas is the perpetual man to beat in tournaments.

"I believe in using confidence baits. If you start out trying some unfamiliar bait, and you throw it for an hour or two without a bite, naturally you start thinking, 'I ought to be throwing a worm,' or whatever your favorite bait is," Shuffield says.

"Well, you probably should have started with the worm in the first place. Confidence is such a major part of successful fishing. There's no reason to handicap yourself

Having Faith
Confidence can be enough justification for pros to use a lure at any given time. A spinnerbait may be the king of confidence baits for both pros and amateurs.

How Shuffield Picks 'Em

1. "When the sky's overcast, bass are usually aggressive, so I rely more on the spinnerbait and crankbait. But under a bright sky, they pull into cover, so then I turn to the worm or jig."

2. "In clear water, I'll fish deeper and with a little more finesse, switching to smaller lures and more subtle actions. But in muddy water, I do the reverse: I fish shallower and with bigger baits that have plenty of action and noise."

3. "When I'm working grasslines, I'll fish a worm along the outer edge, and if I don't get any bites, I'll come down the line again and flip a jig back 2 or 3 feet into the holes."

4. "For worm fishing, I match my sinker size to the time of year. In spring, I like a small weight, 1/8 or 3/16 ounce. But in summer, when I'm usually fishing deeper water and larger worms, I'll go up to a 3/8- or even a 1/2-ounce weight."

5. "Frequently, I use a worm or jig to establish the depth the bass are holding, then I'll try this same depth with a crankbait or spinnerbait. But if I don't get any action on these, I'll go back to the slower bait and stay with it."

by using something you're not 100 percent sure you can catch fish on."

Baits on Shuffield's confidence list include a spinnerbait, crankbait (diving and lipless), jig-and-pig and plastic worm. "I can cover just about all options with these baits. If the bass are chasing shad, I can catch them on the spinnerbait or crankbait. Or if they're sticking tight to structure, I'll get them on the jig or worm.

"I'll fish other baits from time to time, like jerkbaits or topwaters. But these are my standbys. I use them to do the majority of my catching throughout the year."

RON SHUFFIELD believes that lure choice is a confidence game. Instead of trying a lot of different lures, he sticks to a few tried-and-true baits and colors.

Within this overall framework, Shuffield leaves room for variety in terms of bait size, spinnerbait blade size, lure color, etc. He also picks baits according to a seasonal outline that has proved its validity over years of testing.

"In fall, bass follow baitfish into the creeks, and they roam in search of food," he says. "So I hunt for the shad and try to find the depth they are holding and the type cover they're around. Then I match my bait to that set of conditions. For example, the shad might be holding around a grassbed that's 15 feet down. In this case, I'd try a crankbait that would run in the 10- to 15-foot range, or maybe a spinnerbait slow rolled right over the top of the grass. Or I might try a Zara Spook early in the morning over the grass if I see bass pushing shad to the surface."

In shallower areas, Shuffield casts a buzzbait (if he sees surface activity) or a lipless crankbait. If he gets no action on these "power baits," he shifts back to the

KNOWING WHAT to throw starts with knowing where the fish are. When fishing deep water, depthfinders can make lure selection a breeze. If bass are relating to the bottom, soft plastics would be the bait to use. If fish are suspended in the middle of the water column, spoons are a good option. Fish relating to deep cover will probably fall for a crankbait.

worm or jig, fishing them into wood cover like treetops and logs, or grass edges.

If he can't find shallow bass, then he moves back out and fishes the channel drops, especially bends and stumps or other isolated cover. He uses jigs or worms, or crankbaits that run down to the depth of the main structure.

In other words, Shuffield first makes a mental calculation as to where the bass should be, and he goes there and tries to catch them with both fast and slow baits. If neither works, he moves out deeper and tries again. Because he's confident one of these baits will work if he locates bass, he doesn't continuously rummage through his tacklebox in search of a magic lure. He looks for the magic spot instead.

In spring, Shuffield says, bass can be caught shallow, middepth and deep. "The average fisherman usually targets shallow fish because they (the fishermen) are oriented to objects; they like to be throwing at something rather than sitting in open water. On the other hand, I believe you're better off to target fish that have moved into the middepth range, especially if there's grass in the lake. These fish are most active, plus they're less affected by unstable weather."

Shuffield depends on spinnerbaits, crankbaits and jigs during this stage. "I don't throw plastic until the bass are in a full-blown spawning stage. Then I go to tube jigs or small plastic worms, and I stay with these until midsummer."

In all seasons, Shuffield stays with basic colors

and bait models. "I think colors are more important to fishermen than to fish. I use a few proven colors that have caught bass everywhere I've ever been."

In spinnerbaits, Shuffield prefers white/chartreuse skirts. He normally matches blade size to size of the baitfish. He uses only black, brown or black/blue jigs and trailers. In crankbaits, crawfish color is tops in early spring. Otherwise, Shuffield likes chrome in clear or stained water and firetiger in dingy water. In plastic worms, he casts black or pumpkinseed in spring and shades of blue, red or purple in summer and fall.

Like Daves, Shuffield has his own rules for fishing specific conditions or types of cover.

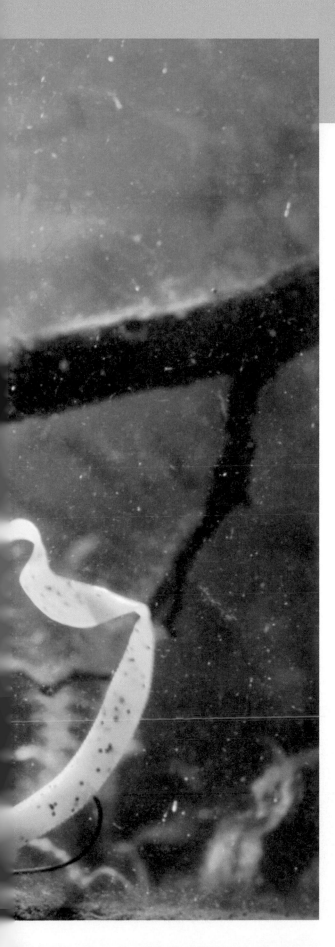

P PLASTICS

Soft, subtle, seductive —
bass find these creations
good enough to eat . . .

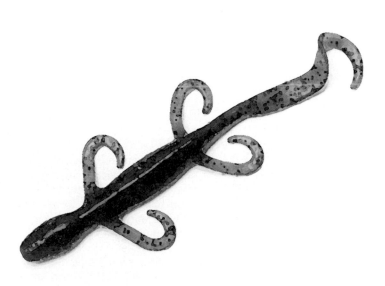

RIGGING PLASTICS THE RIGHT WAY
Advanced rigs for bass baits

THE MOST OVERLOOKED ASPECT of rigging soft plastics has to be the role of the mold mark, says Bruce Benedict, a Texas pro and lure designer.

"Every piece of soft plastic on the market has a mold mark somewhere," he says. "That is where the two halves of the mold come together. There will be a seam on two different sides of every piece of soft plastic, with the exception of tube lures, which are made in a totally different manner.

"Taking the seam into consideration allows that lure to do what it was designed to do — give off the maximum action and attract bass."

Benedict and other seasoned pros provide a detailed look at the proper method for rigging each specific type of soft plastic lure.

SOFT JERKBAITS

Nearly every plastics maker in the industry has followed the Slug-Go lead and now markets some form of this ugly piece of plastic.

But many fishermen don't rig the soft jerkbaits properly and subsequently deprive themselves of the erratic, tantalizing action inherent in these lures.

"The hook has to be perfectly straight in the bait for it to work right," says pro Terry Baksay. "That's what gives the bait that perfect keel effect as it comes through the water. Even if my hook is just a little bit off to the side, I will redo a Slug-Go two or three times to get it right."

Here's how Baksay rigs a soft jerkbait:

1) He inserts a 4/0 or 5/0 wide gap or offset hook directly into the middle of the nose of the lure.

2) After penetrating about 1/2 inch of plastic, he brings the hook out (leaving the eye in the plastic) of the rounded bottom side of the lure.

3) He then rotates the hook into position to re-enter the bait.

4) He bends the bait slightly to enable the hook point to enter the center of the bottom of the jerkbait at a 90 degree angle.

Wacky Worms

The simplest and most unusual of all worm rigs can also be among the most effective, especially when bass are finicky. Simply hook a worm through the egg sac and cast it — without a weight — near shallow cover. Twitch it gently, then let it sink. That's all there is to it.

5) Finally, he pushes the hook through so that the point rests in the small groove on the top of the jerkbait.

FLIPPING/PITCHING WORMS

They come in all shapes, sizes and names, but most of the plastic worms used for flipping/pitching have common characteristics that include a short design, bulky or large diameter body and a stout, C-shaped tail. That shape is best suited for getting the best penetration and maximum vibration in heavy-cover situations. It is designed to be fished on a 3/0 to 5/0 hook and 20-pound-test line or heavier.

"The biggest consideration with rigging this kind of worm is to position the hook so that the worm's short, curled tail is in the down position as it swims through the water," Benedict believes.

Making the worm ride tail down in the water simply involves rigging the hook on the mold mark that is in line with the inside curl of the tail.

Here's a step-by-step look at rigging a heavy-cover worm:

1) Enter through the nose of the worm and exit the hook directly on the proper seam about 3/8 inch down.

2) Slide the worm up to cover the knot and make it more weedless.

3) Rotate the hook and pinch the worm slightly to re-enter the worm.

4) Slide the hook completely through the body of the worm at a 45 degree angle.

5) Tuck the hook point back into the top of the worm (making it weedless but with little plastic to penetrate on the hook set).

THE TEXAS RIG came of age about the same time B.A.S.S. tournaments were first being held in the late 1960s. Since the early days, anglers have devised all sorts of rigging techniques for various lures, presentations and applications.

SOFT JERKBAIT

FLIPPING-STYLE WORM

FLOATING WORM

SWIMMING-TAIL WORM

TEXAS RIG RINGWORM

18-36"

CAROLINA RIG WORM

TUBE JIG WITH INTERNAL WEIGHT

TUBE JIG WITH EXTERNAL WEIGHT

TEXAS RIG GRUB

18-36"

CAROLINA RIG GRUB

GRUB WITH JIGHEAD

SWIMMING-STYLE WORMS

Swimming-style worms are more slender in shape than flipping-type worms and feature a longer, thinner curl or ribbonlike tail.

There are two ways to properly rig this style of worm, depending on how much action is desired. Rigged with the tail up, the worm has less action and is better suited for a methodical retrieve in cover, sometimes referred to as *deadsticking a worm*. Rigged with the tail below as it moves through the water, the worm displaces more water (which means greater vibration) and gets the most out of its built-in action.

Follow the rigging steps detailed under flipping/pitching worms, and either keep the tail up by bringing the hook out of the seam on the top side of the worm, in line with the outer curl of the tail, or exit it on the seam on the inside of the tail to position it down.

TUBE JIGS

Rigging hollow-body tube jigs became considerably easier in the last few years with the advent of wide gap hooks. They enable the lure to be rigged Texas style, but with the hook point slightly exposed. The hook point lays flush on the opposite side of the tube, leaving it uncovered, yet largely weedless.

Tube jigs are usually fished on light line and small diameter hooks. Finesse fishing expert Shaw Grigsby follows these steps when rigging:

1) Insert the hook point into the nose of the tube.

2) Exit the hook about 1/4 inch down.

3) Bring the hook out from the body of the bait and rotate it so that the hook point is facing the lure.

4) Slide the lure up to cover the eye of the hook.

5) Pinch the tube up slightly and insert the hook point straight through the body of the lure (and out the opposite side, where it should rest flat against the plastic).

6) Insert the tip of the hook point just under the skin of the bait to make it even more weedless.

GRUBS

The plastic grub has been around for decades and remains one of the most versatile lures of all. It can be rigged several ways, with the following being two of the most popular:

Texas style — Wide gap hooks greatly enhance our ability to make a grub weedless while still maintaining its effectiveness. Follow the same steps used to rig a tube jig. The result should leave the hook point lying against the side of the plastic, where you can re-enter it just beneath the surface, sometimes referred to as "skin-pricking" it, and make it especially weedless. Be aware that the grub should swim with the curl of its tail downward, so bring the hook out along the mold mark that is in line with the inside of the tail to get the most movement.

Carolina style — Again, the tail should be positioned below the grub as it comes through the water. The hook in a Carolina rig grub can be left exposed in open water or skin-pricked for working cover.

FINESSE WORMS

By their very nature, finesse-type worms are strange creatures. They possess little of the pizazz associated with plastic-worm design. Most are small (3 to 6 inches in length), thin diameter, pencil-shaped worms with straight tails and almost no built-in action.

Finesse worms have a more subtle action, well-suited for inactive bass. Light wire hooks and little or no weight are accessories for the properly dressed finesse worm, which is fished primarily in deep, open water situations.

Unlike injected worms, hand-poured plastics have a flat side. When rigging a hand-poured finesse worm, a Texas rig hook should go in through the flat side and exit the round side. The flat side has a keel effect on the bait, and hooking it in this position gives the worm a more delicate action. When rigging injected worms, line up the hook with either of the two mold marks.

CRAWFISH IMITATIONS

The plastic crawfish is a multipurpose lure. It is productive whether it is Texas rigged for casting and flipping/pitching to shallow cover, rigged Carolina style for deeper situations, or attached as a jig trailer. Regardless of how it is utilized, the most important aspect is something Bruce Benedict refers to as the *eyeball factor.*

"All plastic crawfish have a set of eyeballs, and these baits should always be rigged where the eyes will be in the up position as the bait falls," Benedict explains. "To rig a crawdad to fall properly and have the most action, start the hook point into the plastic about 3/8 inch and bring it out on the belly side of the bait. Rotate the hook and embed it in the body of the crawfish.

"This ensures that the flat section of the claws and the arms of the bait will be in a down position. This is important because you want the arms and claws to swim or move freely as it falls to the bottom. They have more action when the bait falls with the flat side down. It also reduces line twist."

PLASTIC LIZARDS

The rejuvenation of Carolina rigging has brought the plastic lizard back into prominence throughout the country. Long a standard shallow water flipping/pitching tool, the lizard is probably the most popular of all Carolina-style lures.

Lizards offer the same versatility as the imitation crawfish. And the same basic rigging principles apply — particularly the eyeball factor. The bait swims best when the weight of the hook is in the underside of the lure.

Two other tips for rigging plastic lizards:

1) Avoid the tendency to overweight the bait by using a hook that is too large.

2) Run the hook completely through the thick plastic, and then tuck the point back into the top side of the lizard. It will remain weedless, but the hook point is freed instantly upon the hook set.

Rigging plastics the right way is a practice that even some tournament pros haven't mastered. By following these rigging steps, even the most inexperienced angler can be sure that his plastic creatures are functioning exactly as they were designed to perform.

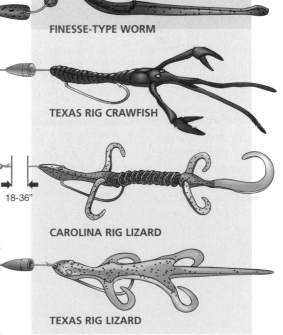

FINESSE-TYPE WORM

TEXAS RIG CRAWFISH

18-36"

CAROLINA RIG LIZARD

TEXAS RIG LIZARD

LIZARD FISHING LESSONS
Bass hate salamanders, so anglers love lizards

TO US, plastic lizards look like little more than fat worms with legs. But bass see them as something much more sinister, and that's why fish attack them with such vengeance. These versatile baits work as well in thick vegetation as they do in stump filled reservoirs.

WHAT DOES THE PLASTIC LIZARD imitate? When should you fish it? How do you rig a lizard? And where should you fish it?

Answers to these questions and more will help any Bassmaster become a better all-around angler.

Although they are called "lizards," these soft plastic lures are meant to imitate salamanders. Of all the species of reptiles and amphibians with that same basic, "four-legs-and-a-tail" body shape, only the tiger salamander in its adult and larval forms would be available as forage for bass, herpetologists tell us.

Tiger salamanders are amphibians, not reptiles, and they begin life as an egg laid in the water in spring. The eggs hatch, and the larvae soon grow into lizard-looking creatures, sometimes called waterdogs, complete with a rounded, finlike tail, four legs and three pairs of external gills at the neck.

For a period of months, the waterdogs live in the shallows of lakes or streams, eating insects while they gradually lose their tail fin (but retain a rounded tail) and gills and turn into adult salamanders.

Once the waterdogs lose their gills, and thus their ability to extract oxygen from the water, they become

creatures of the land, inhabiting dark, moist environments along the shore. These adults are terrestrial salamanders, often called "spring lizards" by live-bait anglers.

In spring, adult salamanders migrate to water for spawning. Their eggs hatch into small waterdogs, which grow quite rapidly. In areas inhabited by tiger salamanders, this places a large number of salamanders in the shallows already filled with prespawn and spawning bass. The results are predictable.

As opportunistic predators, the bass take full and immediate advantage of these easy meals. Live waterdogs and spring lizards are tremendously productive live-bait offerings in virtually every body of water across America. It makes not one whit of difference whether these creatures inhabit the waters or not, bass still will fight to get to them. Consequently, it

makes sense that an imitation salamander or waterdog also would be effective across the country, a fact proved by today's traveling tournament professionals.

For generations, bass anglers have insisted that bass eat — or strike to kill — salamanders because the

Lizard Soup

When fishing water that more closely resembles soup than something you'd drink, consider replacing your plastic worm with a lizard. Although bass won't be able to see the difference, they will be able to feel the extra vibration and water displacement created by the baits' extra appendages. This may be enough extra action to help hungry bass find your bait.

High Floating Lizards

Before Slug-Gos, Senkos and other soft plastic jerkbaits and stickbaits, fishermen were already using a deadly floating plastic bait in shallow water: the floating lizard. Molded of air-enriched plastic, these high floating lizards would twitch and dance across the surface of the water like a swimming salamander.

The few anglers who knew to use them mopped up.

Buoyant lizards are back in a variety of forms, including Yum's Air Lizards, Larew's floating lizards and — newest of all — Cyberflexxx superplastic lizards, such as Terminator's SnapBack brand. When first introduced, SnapBack and similar superplastic baits were touted for being virtually indestructible. But anglers quickly recognized an even more attractive quality: they are extremely buoyant. The photos on this page, courtesy of Outdoor Innovations, clearly demonstrate that characteristic.

In spawning season, a Texas rigged floating lizard looks like a salamander feeding nose-down on the bottom, perhaps gobbling bass eggs. Fished behind a Carolina rig weight, the lizard rides high in the water, easily attracting the attention of any nearby bass.

creatures eat the bass' eggs, and the fish have an instinctive hatred of them. That sounds logical and would provide convenient answers to otherwise puzzling questions, but it is simply not true. Salamanders and waterdogs prey on insects. Bass eat salamanders and waterdogs not out of hate or fear, but for the same reason they eat shad, bream, shiners or crawfish — to fill their gluttonous bellies.

Plastic lizards are generally considered springtime baits and, in fact, many tournament anglers will throw a plastic lizard in lieu of a worm throughout spring.

"In the natural scheme of things, bass see more waterdogs in the spring than they do at any other time," says Tony Watson, a well-versed bass angler from Eufaula, Ala. "Salamanders spawn in the spring about the same time that the bass spawn, and when the eggs hatch, the little waterdogs are all over the shallows."

A firm believer in the match-the-hatch school of thought, Watson throws a synthetic salamander when live salamanders are most available to the bass.

Every angler interviewed for this story believes that plastic lizards are most effective during spring. Buford, Ga., pro Tom Mann Jr. says the baits are also good in summer months, while Lonnie Stanley of Stanley Jigs fame reports a better success rate in fall than summer. And all anglers agreed that the lizards are a poor choice for winter angling.

As with plastic worms, there are scores of ways to fish plastic lizards. The majority of salamander slingers, however, use three basic rigs to cover the lake from top to bottom.

TEXAS STYLE

The Texas rig lizard is a Stanley mainstay. The Texas pro was using lizards long before he developed his jig fishing prowess.

"I'll get twice as many bites on a plastic worm as I will on a lizard, but when the day is finished, the lizard fish will weigh more than the worm fish — even though there may be half as many of them. I think it has to do with the bulk of the lure and the big bait/big bass theory.

"Because a lizard is bulkier than a worm, it draws strikes from larger fish. You can also compare a jig and a lizard in the same manner," he says. "You will get about twice as many bites on a lizard as you will on a jig, but the jig fish will weigh more."

When the fish move shallow in the spring, Stanley often uses a small, 4- to 5-inch, Texas rig lizard coupled with a 1/16- to 1/8-ounce pegged bullet weight.

"A small lizard worked around most any structure will draw strikes, and it is especially effective on bedding bass," he notes, adding that the bulky body of the typical plastic lizard is ideal for the insertion of a worm rattle, a tip he recommends when fishing off-color water. And he says that a Texas rig lizard is a great bait for flipping and pitching.

BASS TYPICALLY ANNIHILATE plastic lizards, especially in spring, but in other times of the year as well. When fish have grown overly accustomed to plastic worms, a lizard offers a different and sometimes more attractive profile.

CAROLINA STYLE

For many years, anglers in Georgia and Alabama have rigged lizards in the Carolina rig style. Tom Mann Jr. calls the rig "a fabulous structure fishing bait that produces far larger fish, on the average, than do-nothing worms."

Most often, Mann rigs his baits with a 1-ounce weight and a 3-foot leader. "This rig is great for fishing relatively clean structure like long bars and points in lakes like West Point," he says, referring to the popular impoundment on the Georgia-Alabama border.

When fishing cover-rich structure like stumpfields and grassbeds, Mann shortens the leader to about 12 inches and switches to a smaller 1/4- to 5/8-ounce sinker.

"In grass, you lose your sense of feel with the long leader, and a big sinker will constantly hang in the bottom cover. This lighter rig (often referred to as the Eufaula rig) will keep you in touch with the lizard and let you spend more time fishing rather than tying on new rigs."

Tony Watson of Eufaula, Ala., also prefers a Carolina rig lizard. Instead of inserting the hook into the lizard's head, as he would when Texas rigging the bait, Watson inserts the hook into the neck of the bait.

"Whenever I lift the line, it picks up the lizard's head, and I think this provides an extremely natural presentation."

TOPWATER TERROR

The plastic lizard is not limited to the bottom of the pond but is also effective as a surface or subsurface lure. Robert Tucker, a bass guide and tournament angler from Houston, Texas, swears by a floating lizard.

"It really is a deadly tactic," he says. "It's not a bait, it's a weapon!"

When Tucker rigs the bait, he pulls the eye of the hook down into the lizard's neck, running the line

through the lizard's head. Then, as he works it across the surface, atop a weedbed or beside a stump, he can keep the lizard's head out of the water by simply raising his rod tip.

Any of the plastic lizards can be fished as subsurface baits by simply rigging them Texas style, sans the sinker. A plastic lizard undulating just under the surface around virtually any structure will draw strikes whenever the bass are in shallow water.

Scores of plastic lizards are currently on the market, and most will catch fish. But for a variety of reasons, each angler has his favorite. Watson prefers the small, 4- to 5-inch lizard, while Mann likes a 6-inch bait.

Color choice in plastic lizards is solely a matter of personal preference, but many of the pros interviewed favor darker hues of brown, pumpkinseed and black. Mann recommends choosing the color according to water clarity and the amount of sunlight — "just as you normally choose a worm color." He says plastic lizards are more productive in clearer water than in murky conditions.

"A lizard is a great visual bait. It's something the fish are accustomed to seeing (in many, but not all, lakes and streams), he says, and it is much more natural to the fish than a plastic worm. I believe that if the bass can see a lizard, they'll hit it more often than they will a plastic worm."

PLASTIC LIZARDS can be fished in any technique with which you'd present a plastic worm. The lizard's extra appendages displace more water as the bait is moved or as it drops through the water, providing extra attraction in off-color water. Lizards are the baits of choice for Carolina riggers, but they work well when rigged Texas style and flipped or pitched to cover.

PLASTIC BODY JIGS can be used in so many different situations — wherever bass are feeding on baitfish. Lures with wide curled tails, like these fat-body grubs, can be hopped off the bottom, or fished in a steady, swimming motion at the fish's level.

(Opposite page) PROBABLY NO lure type has caught more smallmouth bass than the lowly plastic grub. Its compact shape, lifelike texture and subtle movements replicate the bronzeback's favorite foods.

TRENDS IN GRUBBIN'
New tricks for an old bait

ALTHOUGH GRUBS HAVE BEEN AROUND for nearly three decades, they have evolved dramatically in recent years. Manufacturers are offering exciting new versions of these time-tested lures, and top pro anglers and guides are finding new ways of fishing them. To get the inside scoop, BASSMASTER talked with some of the top guns in grubbin'. We think their insights will generate new excitement in grub fishing for you.

BIGGER & FATTER

Smallmouth experts, known for being obsessively picky when it comes to lure preferences, latched on to grubs big-time more than 20 years ago and haven't let go since. These twist-tail soft plastics have arguably caught more smallies in the past two decades than all other bass lures combined. And while lunker largemouth hunters seldom fish grubs, they're the lures of choice for those who seek a trophy smallmouth.

In fact, the biggest bronzeback taken anywhere in the past decade, Paul Beal's 10-pound, 8-ounce monster caught in 1986 from Dale Hollow Reservoir, was caught on a "lowly" 4-inch smoke grub.

Three- and 4-inch Twisters traditionally have been the gold standard for smallies. But lately, even hard-core bronzebackers like Tennessee guides Jack Christian and Fred McClintock have seen their grub preferences shift. Both Christian, who guides on Priest Lake, and McClintock, who guides on Dale Hollow, have switched to bigger, fatter grubs in the past few years.

"The only grubs I used for 15 years were 3-inchers in smoke or pumpkin," Christian says. "But when manufacturers began offering the fat-bodied 4- and 5-inchers a few years back, I experimented with them and liked what I found. From a guide's standpoint, a 3-inch grub is a great 'numbers' lure. Your client gets a lot of bites when using it, and he stands the chance of catching

Grub Jigs

The style of jighead used has a huge impact on how and where grubs will be most effective. (Top) Football heads are great for hopping over rocky bottoms; their shape causes the lure to wag from side to side. (Middle) Darter head jigs are superb finesse baits; Western bass anglers like to shake them vertically through deep schools of bass. (Bottom) Ball head jigs are an all-around style that can be used for hopping, swimming or crawling down stairstep ledges.

Advanced Grubbin' Tips

COLORS — Use silver, smoke or clear grubs on sunny days; white or chartreuse in murky water or on overcast days; and pumpkinseed colors wherever smallmouth live and where bass feed on crawfish.

JIG RIGS — When fishing a grub on a jighead, rig so the hook point is in line with the ridge of the curled tail; this will minimize line twist. Grubs with flat tails can be rigged with the tail perpendicular to the bottom for a fast fall and good swimming action, or parallel to the bottom for a tantalizing gliding motion.

WORMS RIGS — Grubs make great lures for Carolina rigging, Texas rigging and split shotting. Use a wide gap hook on a 4- or 5-inch fat-body grub. For easier hook sets, insert the hook barb all the way through the grub body so it lies flat with the top of the grub, then skin-hook the point in the top of the bait.

TRAILERS — Grubs make great trailers for hard lures; their soft texture makes bass hold on longer. On rubber legged jigs, use double-curled-tail grubs; on spinnerbaits, use a single-curled-tail model or a straight-tail grub.

OPEN HOOKS — Grubs can be fished on Texas rigs, with a worm-style hook buried in the plastic. But they provide surer hook sets on light line when fished on jigheads with exposed hooks.

a trophy smallmouth as well. But when I tried the larger sizes, I discovered the overall quality of the fish we caught went up, while our total numbers of bass didn't decline greatly."

"The 5-inch fat grubs are definitely a great choice for lunker smallies," McClintock agrees, "but I like them best in the spring, when the water is above 55 degrees. In winter, I get more consistent action on smaller, thinner grubs. Bass want a very compact meal in cold water."

Both guides agree that smallmouth bass take fat-body grubs with a vengeance. "There's no question when she's got it," Christian says. "You feel a very distinct tap when a smallie inhales a fat grub. They're considerably softer than standard grubs, and must feel totally real when the bass inhales it. They eat it without hesitation, just like living prey."

TIP OF THE ICEBERG

"The grub has traditionally been a hard sell to the largemouth fisherman everywhere but the West," says Al Kalin of the Kalin Co., a Brawley, Calif., manufacturer of soft plastic lures, including bass grubs. "In highly pressured Western waters, finesse anglers have relied on grubs for largemouths for years, but in Middle America and the South, there is still some resistance to them."

What do western anglers know about grubs that fishermen elsewhere may not? "The grub is easily the most versatile lure in your tacklebox," Kalin asserts. "You can fish it on a leadhead and, by varying the weight, probe virtually any depth zone. But rigging it on a leadhead is just the tip of the iceberg."

Oklahoma bass pro Ken Cook is one of the biggest advocates of grubbin'. He agrees that the number of ways the lure can be fished is almost unlimited. "You can do more with a grub than any other soft plastic bait," he says. "Everybody wants to fish it on a leadhead . . . don't get me wrong, that's a great tactic at times . . . but I've learned to fish grubs literally from top to bottom."

As a case in point, Cook reveals how he fishes a grub in dense weedbeds: "A grub is a tremendous vegetation lure when rigged Texas style (with a worm sinker, glass bead and hook point hidden) and pitched or flipped into trash," he explains. "I use it in midsummer, when bass are on a shad bite. A grub's size and action closely match that of a live baitfish. As it slithers down through the grass, the tail has a subtle, slow-swinging action, which projects a convincing shad profile."

Cook likes a 6-inch grub rigged with an extra-wide gap 4/0 hook for short-line presentations into vegetation. "The fat body of a big grub demands a short, wide-bite worm hook. A standard worm hook just won't cut it."

The extra bulk of the grub's body calls for "skin-hooking": "Stick the point of the hook all the way through the lure, then back it into the skin on the very outside of the body. This keeps the grub weedless so it can crawl through grass, but allows the point to penetrate the jaw of the bass easily when you set the hook."

WEIGHTED WAYS

Besides fishing them in grass, Cook routinely Carolina rigs a grub. "I use a grub almost as much as a lizard for this application," he explains. "A grub rigged Carolina style is a dynamite 'search' lure, especially in the fall, when bass key heavily on shad. I use it to comb a wide area quickly. But for some reason it hasn't caught on with Bassmasters who use this popular rigging approach the way a lizard or worm has."

Neither worms nor lizards have the grub's strong resemblance to a baitfish, Ken believes. "It's my lure of choice when Carolina rigging in clear water. This is a tremendous 'numbers' approach. You'll catch an unbelievable number of keeper bass on it." Depending on size of the fish and water clarity, Cook recommends either a 4- or 6-inch grub on the business end of your Carolina leader.

"Western anglers have used grubs on a split shot rig for years," says lure maker Kalin. "This technique is easy to use and catches a lot of fish."

There are numerous variations for split shot rigging, but most finesse experts would agree on this starting point: Use a medium action 6-foot spinning rod and light line. Rig the grub of your choice Texas style with a sharp worm hook, then pinch a single BB-sized split shot on the line about 18 inches from the lure.

Cast, let the shot hit bottom and point the rod tip at the water's surface. Then either start reeling slowly and constantly, or, with rod tip pointed at the water, sweep the tip back and to the side, slowly enough so the shot maintains bottom con-

tact. Return the rod to the start position while reeling up slack, then sweep back again. The split shot technique is ideal in clear lakes lacking dense cover.

ADDED ATTRACTION

A grub can be a great trailer for a jig or spinner-bait, Cook has found. He especially recommends a grub trailer on a spinnerbait where the water is murky to muddy, when you want to 'float' the lure over the top of submerged grassbeds, and whenever you're gunning for lunker bass.

Increasingly, Cook has been tipping his weed-less flipping and pitching jigs with grubs when fishing submerged wood.

He believes one reason a grub is so deadly as a jig trailer results from its ability to entice a strike even when the lure is sitting still. "The grub's thin, feathery tail will undulate with the slightest water movement. A bass swimming up to examine a grub will disturb the water just enough to move the tail; this often draws an instant strike, for the lure appears alive to the fish."

TOPWATER TEASER

Those who have fished grubs only on leadheads in the past will be especially shocked to learn they're being touted as surface lures. "Our 6-inch Mogambo grub can be fished on top like a buzzbait," claims Kalin. "Rig it weedless on a 4/0 offset worm hook. Cast the lure around grass or wood cover as you would a buzzbait, then retrieve it quickly so the tail flaps on the surface."

These tips from our experts are aimed at getting grubs out of the bottom of your tacklebox and putting them where they belong — in the top drawer. As Ken Cook says, "If you're not fishing grubs, you're missing out on a whole lot of strikes — and a barrel of fun besides."

YOU'LL NEED spinning tackle to fish plastic grubs, especially in the sizes favored by smallmouth bass. Open-face reels are just right for small diameter lines, which allow grubs to swim and move naturally in deep water.

EVER SINCE Nick Crème molded the first soft plastic worm, bass fishermen have been proving how versatile and effective these artificial lures can be.

THE ART OF WORM FISHING
Venerable plastic worm continues its fish catching legacy

IF RENOWNED BASS ANGLER Larry Nixon were forced to choose one lure for the remainder of his fishing days, there would be no indecision. He would immediately select the 6-inch plastic worm. He credits this lure for his enduring success, and claims it vaulted him to the

2002 CITGO BASS Masters Classic on Alabama's Lay Lake.

"The worm has been my favorite lure since I began fishing it more than 35 years ago," says Nixon. "The first plastic worms I ever saw were made by Gilmore. We rigged them on weedless

throw," says Nixon. "We didn't know anything about pattern fishing and throwing different lures at different times."

Over the ensuing years, Nixon has amassed winnings of $1.5 million in B.A.S.S. tournaments alone, including 14 career wins, two Angler-of-the-Year titles, and 23 berths to the Classic. He relied on a worm to win the Classic on the Ohio River in 1983.

STRAIGHT WORM

Nixon has caught bass on all sizes and styles of plastic worms, and he continues to do so. But he favors a plain, straight-tail, 6-inch worm above all others. Many anglers, to their own detriment, no longer use this venerable design. The 6-inch worm appeals to bass of all sizes. It draws strikes when bass are aggressive, and also when they are in a funk.

"When fishing gets tough, a straight 6-inch worm is always my go-to bait," says Nixon. "It has a more natural, subtle fall than swimming-tail worms. A swimming tail acts as a rudder. A straight-tail worm falls more erratically. That's a triggering mechanism."

Berkley's 6-inch Carolina Power Crawler does the heavy lifting for Nixon these days. Don't let the word 'Carolina' throw you. Nixon dotes on this worm for Texas and Carolina riggings. He believes it coaxes a feeding bite, as opposed to a reaction strike.

STRAIGHT SHANK HOOK

Straight shank worm hooks were the only option when Nixon began fishing the Texas rig. Though most anglers have switched to offset worm hooks, Nixon still prefers the straight shank for Texas rigging. He relies on a 2/0 Gamakatsu hook when fishing 6-inch worms. The exception is when he is fishing a Carolina rig, in which case he switches to an offset worm hook.

"I use a straight shank hook because I don't miss as many bass with it," says Nixon. "When I set the hook, the worm slides down the shank, and the point pops right through the plastic."

Nixon acknowledges that worms don't last as

A 6-INCH FLOATING worm produces bites for Mike Auten whenever bass are shallow, but he fares best with it through the spawning season.

jigheads. That was around 1966, before I learned about the Texas rig."

When Nixon tried his first Texas rigged worm at Arkansas' Greers Ferry Lake in 1969, it was love at first bite. Here was a bait that worked equally well in the shallows as in the depths; penetrated the thickest cover without a hitch; and tempted bass with a lifelike, almost irresistible action. Over the next several years, Nixon, and the bass fishing world in general, came down with worm mania.

"In those days, the worm was the *only* bait to

Worm Trailers

Both Larry Nixon and Mike Auten use 6-inch worms, or portions of them, to dress weedless bass jigs. Auten prefers a worm with a large action tail, such as a Gatortail Worm. He may use the whole worm, or cut off 2 inches of the worm's head.

"That big Gatortail grabs a lot of water and slows the jig's fall," says Auten. "I use it most often when I'm flippin' to holes in grass."

Nixon pinches off the last 4 inches of 6-inch ribbontail worms and tips jigs with them during the summer months.

"When I'm fishing 15 feet or deeper in the summertime, a slim worm trailer gives the jig a straighter, faster fall," says Nixon. "It saves time getting to the bottom, and a lot of times, that fast fall is what makes bass bite."

LARRY NIXON mastered worm fishing on Toledo Bend Reservoir on the Texas-Louisiana border, and he has refined it on countless lakes, rivers and reservoirs throughout the United States.

long on straight shank hooks as on offset hooks. But his emphasis is on catching bass, not getting the most mileage out of every worm. However, if you use worms that are so soft they refuse to stay put on a straight shank hook, Nixon concedes that an offset hook is the only option. He prefers worms that have enough substance to grip a straight shank hook.

A 1/8- or 3/16-ounce Lake Fork Mega-Weight bullet sinker gets the call most often when Nixon fishes a 6-inch worm. He avoids pegging the sinker whenever possible, because he is convinced that a free-sliding weight allows for a better hook set. When he must work the worm into dense limbs or heavy weeds, Nixon pegs the sinker with a toothpick or a rubber band.

BACK OFF

When fishing worms around shallow, visible targets, many anglers immediately get close and dissect it with flippin' and pitchin' presentations. While close-quarter fishing does improve accuracy, Nixon believes this approach bypasses boatloads of bass.

"When you flip and pitch, you normally don't fish cover under water that you can't see," says Nixon. "I cast from a little farther back and keep fishing the worm as long as I can feel anything that might hold fish. Besides, somebody may have already plucked bass off the obvious cover. When you work farther away, you fish water other guys miss."

A sensitive rod is crucial when casting worms. Nixon dotes on a Fenwick 6-foot,

Worm Styles

Curled Tail — These worms drop relatively slowly and put out a subtle vibration.

Ribbon — Ribbon-tail worms' thin tails wobble wildly and attract bass visually.

Flipping — Fairly thick and made of tougher plastic, flipping worms accommodate the stout hooks needed in flipping and pitching techniques.

Ribbed — These "ring worms" displace water and send out extra vibrations, making them effective in weeds as well as off-color water.

Finesse — Usually 4 inches long and sporting a straight tail, finesse worms are fished on light line when bass are not very active. Can be fished on Texas, Carolina, split shot and drop shot rigs.

Floating — Rig Texas style on a 4/0 hook and without a weight, twitch on the surface around docks, weeds and brush.

6-inch, Techna AV high modulus graphite rod in medium-heavy action. He matches the rod with a 6:1 gear ratio Abu Garcia low profile reel and 10- to 14-pound Trilene XT line.

"My goal in fishing is to get as many bites as I possibly can," says Nixon. "I get many more worm bites with light line."

Nixon also gets more bites on long casts, especially in clear water. He believes many anglers put bass off by crowding them. No, you can't pick cover apart with long casts, but when bass are holding to the edges of cover, Nixon fares better from 60 feet than 30 feet.

SEARCH BAIT

You may be surprised to learn that Nixon also uses a Texas rigged worm as a search lure, a job normally reserved for the likes of spinnerbaits and crankbaits.

"Some guys say you can't cover water fast enough with a worm," says Nixon. "That's hogwash. I can cover as much water with a worm as you can with a spinnerbait. I keep the boat moving, and cast to key pieces of cover. I hop it a few times, reel in and make the next cast. There are times when bass will not move to take a spinnerbait."

One of those times was when Nixon won the Classic on the Ohio River. The bass were not reacting to moving baits, and Nixon had to search with a Texas rigged worm for every bass he caught. He faced a similar situation when he won a MegaBucks event on Florida's Harris Chain.

WHOOP SNAP

When casting a worm, Nixon maintains a high hooking percentage using what he calls a "Whoop Snap." The instant he feels a bass tap, he drops the rod tip about 8 inches, snap-sets hard against the semislack line, cranks like a maniac until the line tightens, and sets the hook again to ensure the barb is buried. Should a bass strike close to the

MIKE AUTEN skips a 6-inch floating worm to shallow cover. Note the spinning tackle, which is conducive to skipping the light bait.

boat, he avoids the Whoop Snap, because it could break his line. In this instance, he goes with more of a sweep set, which pulls the hook into the bass.

FLIP AND PITCH

If Nixon has no choice but to dig bass out of dense labyrinths with a flippin' or pitchin' rod, he switches to a 6-inch Ribbontail Power Worm, a stout, offset Gamakatsu Superline Worm Hook, a pegged 5/16- or 3/8-ounce bullet sinker, and 17- to 25-pound-test Trilene XT.

"A bulkier ribbontail worm drops straight down into cover and gives you more control," says Nixon. "A straight-tail worm winds around when it falls. When you fish heavy cover, water displacement is much more important than a bait that looks totally realistic. Bass feel the vibration of a ribbontail worm. They respond with a reflex strike."

Nixon prefers dark worms, including junebug, black, black with chartreuse tail and purple, when probing cover. In open water, he opts for junebug, black grape, blue grape, purple, pumpkin chartreuse, and pumpkinseed.

Kentucky's Mike Auten, a three time Classic

THE ORIGINAL TEXAS rigged worm was made to order for heavily timbered reservoirs. Virtually snag proof, they could be worked through the thickest tangles of brush and limbs without hanging up. Because the hook is not exposed, a hard hook set with a stiff action rod is required. In the early days of worm fishing, newcomers to the technique were advised to "cross his eyes" when setting the hook.

qualifier, wasn't around to witness the birth of the plastic worm. Even so, he also sings the praises of the 6-incher. He regularly fishes them Texas style with a 3/0 offset Gamakatsu Wide Gap Worm Hook. He does well casting straight worms, but also alternates them with ribbon-tail and curled-tail worms.

ACTION WORMS

"I change worms to give bass a different look," says Auten. "A straight worm falls fast, with a darting action. Ribbon-tail worms (such as the Culprit) drop straight and appeal to bass with their wiggling tails. Curled-tail worms (such as the Mr. Twister) fall slowly and put out a different vibration. That flopping curled-tail works almost like a big Colorado blade on the back of a worm."

Auten goes with a curled-tail worm whenever he wants to give bass more time to look the bait over. A 1/16- or 1/8-ounce slip sinker accentuates the slow decent. He also rigs the curled-tail worm on a light jighead with an exposed hook when fishing off the edges of grasslines. Few bass can resist the jig's subtle hop-drop action.

WACKY WORM

In the spring, Auten shows bass an even slower drop when he rigs a straight 6-inch worm wacky style by impaling the bait's egg sac with a straight shank 3/0 worm hook. He flings the light offering next to flooded bushes and shallow grass, and works it with twitches and pauses. When twitched, both ends of the bait fold back and spring out. During pauses, each end of the worm undulates seductively as the bait sinks — just the thing for drawing bass out of cover.

"As with all fishing, you have to pay attention to the mood of the bass," says Auten. "Sometimes they want that wacky worm fished real slow, with long pauses that let the bait sink down out of sight."

SPEED WORMING

Auten's most upbeat worm fishing tactic, called speed worming, also does well in the spring. He learned this method from local anglers during a guiding stint on fabled Lake Okeechobee. The bait consists of a 6-inch Gambler paddle-tail worm rigged Texas style with a 3/0 or 4/0 offset worm hook. It is imperative that the edge of the paddle-tail be aligned vertically on the hook, like a keel. Auten normally uses speed worms without a weight, but will add a 1/16- or 1/8-ounce bullet sinker if a breeze kicks up. However, this is not a technique for windy conditions.

"Cast the worm in shallow vegetation like pads, peppergrass and Kissimmee grass," says Auten. "Then reel it almost like a spinnerbait. The worm's paddle-tail flutters wildly back and forth, like a propeller. That's part of the attraction. Bass blow up on it like they do on a buzzbait.

A Quantum Tour Edition 6-foot, 6-inch, medium-heavy rod with a Quantum E600 6.3:1-gear ratio reel is Auten's choice for speed worming. He typically goes with Stren 12-pound test or heavier line.

FLOATING WORM

Auten takes shallow bass on a 6-inch floating worm spring through fall, but gives the bait its highest priority when bass cruise before they begin nesting, when they are on the beds, and when they guard fry after the spawn. A bubblegum Zoom Trick Worm is his primary player, though he also switches to black or white to throw bass a change-up.

Auten carefully rigs the Trick Worm perfectly straight with an offset 4/0 hook. A straight worm reduces line twist and allows Auten to walk the bait back and forth. He prefers not to place a swivel on the line ahead of the worm.

"A floating worm is a stealthy, subtle bait," says Auten. "It is less likely to alarm bass during the spawning period than power-type baits."

The floating worm is also a superior skipping lure, which is another reason Auten is so keen on the bait. It skitters under docks and beneath overhanging cover, and lands so lightly it doesn't spook bass. Only spinning tackle effectively handles this light bait, especially with skipping presentations. Auten wields a 6-foot, 6-inch, Quantum Tour Edition medium-heavy spinning rod and a Quantum E74 reel filled with 12-pound Stren.

"I fish a floating worm under the surface, but I usually keep it in sight," says Auten. "I alternately let it flutter down, then twitch it twice to give it a side-to-side action."

This gambit paid off for Auten a few years ago while fishing a B.A.S.S. tournament at Neely Henry. Many of the bass he caught were spawning or guarding fry on the shady sides of stumps. When he twitched his bubblegum worm through the dark spot, the bass would roll up and take the bait. Auten netted enough bass to finish in the Top 10, and earned enough points to qualify for the Classic that year.

Choosing Worm Hooks

In the early days of worm fishing, anglers had few choices for Texas rigging their plastic worms. The straight shank Southern Sproat hook — similar to the style Larry Nixon uses today — was the standard selection.

Today, dozens of styles are available, and each design has its fans. Most anglers pack two or three different hook designs, including some of the ones shown in the photo above. They are described below, in order

from left to right:

1 Offset Shank Hook — Probably the most popular hook for plastic worms, the bend in the shank helps hold worms in place.

2 Wide Gap — Ideal for thick worms and other types of soft plastics, these prevent the plastic from balling up in the bend and preventing good hook penetration.

3 Round Bend — Proponents believe the oversize bend in these hooks hold fish better. The design is great for floating worms and some soft jerkbaits that are skin-hooked through the top of the plastic.

4 HP Hook — A modified Kahle hook, this design has a clip at the eye to hold tubes, worms and other soft plastics in place.

5 Coated Hook — Some hooks are dipped in Teflon or other slippery substances that are said to aid in hook penetration.

6 Sproat — The original favorite, a straight shank hook, provides good hook sets but is not good at holding the worm's head in place. Straight shank hooks are preferred for wacky rigging and for many finesse worm presentations.

7 Belly Weighted Hook — These are meant for use without additional weight, and they're great when bass want a slow falling worm or other lure.

8 Extra Wide Gap — Similar to the wide gap hook, these are preferred for Carolina rigging and for use with flipping tubes and other thick body plastic baits.

CREATURE BAITS
Add a freak bait to your arsenal

WITH THEIR EXTRA appendages and misplaced heads, they seem better suited for a carnival sideshow than a tacklebox.

Some seem to have been spawned from the marriage of two distinctly separate species, possibly bats and snakes. Others appear to be the mis-shapen survivors of radiation experiments with lizards and crawfish. The "match the hatch" philosophy does not apply here — unless these baits were intended for fishing on Mars.

But forget about how unrealistic these "freak baits" look. They catch fish. Davy Hite proved that when he used one of the monstrosities to help win the 1999 BASS Masters Classic in the Louisiana Delta, and since then, these unsightly soft plastics have been the hottest new lures of the new century.

"This is just an amazing new lure," says Hite of Gambler's Bacon Rind, a creature with bat wings near the head of its ribbed body and flippers on either side of its ribbon tail.

Versatile Lures

Looking like something from outer space, creature baits are distinguished by multiple appendages, including arms, legs, pincers and flapper tails. More versatile than a jig-and-pig, they can be fished Texas style, on a Carolina rig and as a trailer. What's more, they have a knack for catching huge bass.

Ribs, flattened appendages and thicker bodies translate into increased buoyancy and tantalizing action that bass haven't seen before. Realistic movement, in other words, makes one of these baits appear to be a tantalizing morsel, freakish appearance notwithstanding.

"The appendages give the bait a gliding motion

that makes it resemble a crawfish," says Gambler's Russ Bringger of the Bacon Rind.

Hite flipped and pitched the Bacon Rind to win in the Louisiana Delta, and those two techniques generally are most popular for use with freak baits. But now anglers are discovering these lures possess incredible versatility, as well as lifelike action.

"I can take a bag of "It" baits, go down a bank, and fish three or four different situations," says New Jersey pro Mike Iaconelli, a two time Classic contender.

Mann's It consists of a long stem of plastic with four tentacles in front and a pair of flappers on either side of a "creature head" in the rear.

CREATURE BAITS really shine when flipped around lily pads and aquatic vegetation.

AFTER DAVY HITE won the 1999 Classic with Gambler's Bacon Rind creature bait, sales of that and similar soft plastics shot up. Hite's trick was swimming a Texas rigged Bacon Rind between a muck bottom and the underside of floating vegetation mats.

"With all of those appendages, I can make modifications and fish the lure in five or six different ways," Iaconelli says.

Kentucky pro Mark Menendez, meanwhile, prefers YUM's Wooly Single Curl Tail, a freak bait that is less freakish-looking than most, but can be used in a variety of ways nonetheless. "It takes the place of a jig, a buzzbait, a swimming spoon and a scum frog," he says.

"This one bait makes it so much easier. I don't have to carry as much. I can simplify my choices for plastic baits."

With its thick, ribbed body and curly tail, the YUM lure is a "big style bait with a small profile," Menendez adds. "It will give me the same quality bite as a jig."

THE BIRTH OF FREAK BAITS

The versatility of freak baits also is reflected in their origins as Carolina rig offerings.

"We didn't even know it was a flipping bait," says Edward Chambers, who invented Zoom's Brush Hog more than a dozen years ago and believes his freak was the first. "We Carolina rigged it, and it was an awesome, lazy bait."

Wings, or flippers, on the rear of the bait slowed its fall and also gave it an erratic descent. "Then I went with double tails (between the wings) so it would work better as a crawfish imitator," he says.

"Now we've learned that you can do so many things with that bait," Chambers adds. "You can cut off the legs at the front or the back. You can cut off the wings or shred them so they look like a Gitzit.

You can take the double tail off and fish it backward, as a fellow does out on Lake Mead. He says he catches bass that way when they're in the tules."

A cousin to Mann's It, the Dragin' Fly also got its start as a Carolina rig bait. Only then, it was called the Mosquito Hawk and didn't attract much angler attention.

Still, Mississippi angler Chase Ross, a member of Mann's pro staff, enjoyed good success with the winged creature.

"It has a large profile, but it works well for big fish," Ross says. "It has a different appearance from most baits. It looks like a willow fly, and fish like to eat willow flies when they hatch in the lake."

As a flipping bait, he adds, the Dragin' Fly "looks like something that would come out of a tree."

Ross sees no problem using a bait that is considerably bigger than the insect he believes it imitates. "Bass will eat a finesse worm, and they will eat a 13- or 14-inch worm," he says. "It's all the same to bass. It's food. That's why I have confidence in it."

Through experimentation, Iaconelli and Menendez also have gained confidence in their preferred freak baits as year-round offerings for a multitude of patterns. Here's how they fish them:

FREAK BAIT RIGS

First, both emphasize that a wide gap hook is important for fishing freak baits rigged Texas style.

"You have to have a wide gap because you are dealing with more plastic," says Menendez.

"I like a superwide gap offset hook in 3/0 or 4/0," adds Iaconelli.

For flipping, pitching and even casting the Wooly Single Curl Tail, Menendez recommends using screw-in weights of 5/16 to 1/2 ounce and line of 17- to 20-pound test.

Iaconelli uses weights of 3/8 ounce and up for flipping the It. "It's important to peg the weight or use a Gambler screw-in," he says.

The New Jersey pro also performs amputations to make his freak bait better suited to flipping. Removal of the small front appendages, he explains, keeps the bait from sticking to vegetation as it is dropped or dragged.

If conditions such as clear, shallow water dictate a more delicate presentation, he might break off the paddles at the rear of the bait and rig it wacky-worm style with a 2/0 straight-shank hook.

"These types of changes are not specific to the It," he emphasizes. "You can use these tricks with other creature baits as well. Many times, the key to success with these baits is to modify them."

For cast-and-retrieve action, Iaconelli will break off the small side legs of the It and pinch off the head.

"Those paddle tails then will kick together, and it's almost like you are using a spinnerbait with a Colorado blade," he explains. "But it's a vibration the fish have never seen before."

For this "speed worming," Iaconelli rigs Texas style with a smaller weight than he would use for flipping.

Menendez uses a similar technique with the Wooly Curl Tail. "It's great for buzzing the grass," he says. "I've used it anywhere I've found grass, and it's been effective.

"The great thing is that I can penetrate the grass with this bait if I want to, or I can swim it or buzz it. Its bulk has more resistance in the water than most soft plastics, so I can buzz it at a slow speed. It sounds like a small buzzbait when it comes across the water. I never thought I'd fish a plastic like that."

The It, by contrast, doesn't buzz on top — it pops.

"I pinch off the head and fish the bait backward," Iaconelli says. "I Texas rig the hook in the middle of the flappers. With its bulk, I can throw the bait a mile. And it really pushes the water when I bring it back.

"Fish are used to seeing spoons, rats and frogs, but not this."

CAROLINA STYLE

For Carolina rigging, anglers typically turn to smaller versions of the many creature baits on the market.

"With all those appendages, one of these baits takes its time settling to the bottom, which makes it good for Carolina rigging too. I like to go to the 3-inch version to mop up an area," says Menendez.

A critter bait, he adds, also works well as a jig trailer. "If the water is muddy or the fish are aggressive, I'll bite the head off the bait and use the rest," he says. "It puts out more vibration than most trailers."

"These are just real versatile baits," Iaconelli says.

"I suppose you could tie these baits to some specific forage," the New Jersey pro adds. "But it's really the vibration and the silhouettes that make them shine. You've got side arms that quiver, paddle tails, all sorts of things that make them look like something alive."

What Do Bass See?

Lure manufacturers are limited only by their imaginations as they concoct entries into the creature bait category. This Yum Hula Hog is a combination spider grub and freak bait. No one is sure just what bass think they're biting, but fish do seem to love these baits.

WESTERN PATTERNS FOR TUBE BAITS
Tube tricks from West Coast pros

WESTERN PROS prefer a tube bait for flipping and pitching because of its slow vertical fall. Additionally, its compact body eliminates the misses associated with short-striking fish.

IN MANY PARTS OF THE COUNTRY, the tube bait fills a finite niche in the bass angler's arsenal. Most often, it's used as a sight fishing tool for ill-tempered spawners.

Increasingly, however, learned anglers are expanding the role of the tube bait, fishing it as a drop bait in other seasons for suspending bass. And, resourceful bass anglers in the West, where the tube was born, have taken a liking to the diminutive bait, expanding its application to cover all seasons and most situations.

According to lure manufacturer Chris Hendershot, and western bass pros Steve Klein, Russ Meyers, John Murray and Doug Noda, the tube bait is the "go to" bait when the going gets really ugly.

BASSMASTER readers will benefit from the applications these accomplished anglers have developed for this traditionally "tough bite" bait.

Together they explain how the versatile bait is effective, beginning in early spring, throughout summer, and on into winter.

CAROLINA RIGGING TUBES

It's Doug Noda's business to know the hottest trends in lure application for bass fishing, and in the trendy West, that's a full-time job. The tackle distributor explains that one of his favorite uses for the tube bait is dragging it over and around aquatic vegetation.

"On Clear Lake (in northern California)," explains Noda, "we fish a Carolina rig tube bait over the tops and along the outside edges of hydrilla beds. When the bass are holding just above the weedline, you can pull that tube bait over the top of the grass and draw the tough strike."

According to Noda, the latest trick is to use a long, crimp-style weight to deliver the compact package. Similar to a cylindrical Mojo weight, yet

Heads Up

All jigheads are not created equal when fishing tubes. Anglers should opt for a head with a brushguard when fishing vegetation, and a football-style head when rock is prevalent.

Tube Crawling For Smallmouth

Tubes on exposed hooks rival plastic grubs as the most productive and popular smallmouth baits. Lately, anglers in Great Lakes waters have been enjoying tremendous results with the simplest of retrieves: tube crawling.

The technique mimics a crawfish crawling along the bottom. Use a 3- to 4-inch tube, rigged Texas style on a wide gap hook. For crawling in shallow water, pinch a split shot a foot ahead of the tube. In deep water or windy conditions, use a bullet sinker weighing from 1/8 to 3/8 ounce.

When bass are in the shallows, let the lure settle to the bottom, then move it along with your rod tip, pausing to reel in slack. For fishing deep structure where smallies are holding, you might need to move upwind of the target area, let out extra line and drift across the hot spot.

Either way, set the hook when you feel any unusual sensation in the line.

WHEN TEXAS rigging tubes, make sure you use a wide gap hook. The thick body of the bait needs room to compress when fish bite.

A CAROLINA RIGGED TUBE BAIT is a useful tool when bass are holding on top of the grass or along the outside edge.

easier to manage, the crimp-style weight can be adjusted up or down the line and is easier to pull through the grass than a Carolina rig. He rigs the bait weedless, injects a fish attractant, and stuffs a piece of foam packing material into the tube. The foam helps keep the fish attractant in the tube and floats the bait above the grass.

"When the fishing gets real tough," says Noda, "we go to the tube baits. When the fish aren't willing to move for a bigger bait, they often will take the smaller, subtler tube bait. I think it's effective because the bait's compact, and yet more subtle than a grub or a worm."

FLIPPIN' TULES

Many anglers are surprised when they see northern California's Russ Meyers flipping tube baits, rather than jigs or worms. The tournament angler and guide often turns to the compact baits in spring, when bass are relating to relatively shallow cover. According to Meyers, flipping tube baits in spring can produce all day long.

Meyers uses a modified version of the traditional Texas rig. To make setting the hook easier, he punches a hole in the bait for the hook point to penetrate. He uses a 4/0 straight-shank hook, and he pegs the hook eye to the lure with a piece of 40-pound-test monofilament line.

Unlike most of his West Coast peers, Meyers uses little or no weight when flipping tube baits. "Bass tend to shy away from heavier baits in spring," he says. "I don't like to use any weight in spring — and I seldom go higher than 5/32 ounce."

When he does use weight, instead of the traditional sliding worm weight, Meyers prefers split shot. Inserting the hook through the top of the bait, Meyers slides the tube up the line, then crimps a split shot on the line just above the hook. He then slides the tube back over the shot and hook, securing it in place with the monofilament peg.

His favorite spot for flipping tubes is where a fresh growth of tules (reeds) or grass has formed a distinct inside edge between shore and the main weedbed.

"The inside edge is usually free of silt and has a hard bottom," notes Meyers. "Sometimes you have to push back into 30 or 40 yards of cover to reach that inside edge, but it's often worth it."

Meyers fishes inside edges with a weightless tube bait, flipping it into the cover and twitching it. "The primary reason I use tube baits when flipping shallow cover, is because it's a short distance between the tail of the bait to the point of the hook. You seldom miss a fish on a tube bait."

SUMMER SHAD PATTERNS

Arizona's John Murray is gaining a reputation as one of the West's most versatile and accomplished tournament anglers. He finds the tube bait to be a useful tool when bass are chasing shad.

"In summer, when the bass are targeting the larger shad, I have a lot of success using the jumbo tube baits," he says. The Arizona pro believes it's important to match the hatch with tubes, and he often fishes a 4- to 4 1/2-inch tube bait on a 1/8- to 1/4-ounce leadhead jig when the bass are after bigger forage. He positions the jighead about 1/4 inch from the tip of the tube, which causes the bait to slowly circle as it falls.

Murray uses tubes in situations in which other anglers might shake western-style

worms — along steep dropoffs on main lake ridges. Extreme dropoffs are the key to finding bass actively chasing shad schools, according to Murray, who believes bass herd shad against the steep drops.

The pro carefully manages his line as the bait falls, because bass often strike the bait on the fall.

DREDGING THE DEEP

In winter, Steve Klein finds the tube bait to be an effective way to draw strikes from bass hugging deep structure.

"When everyone else is throwing jigs and worm rigs," says the northern California pro, "I'll drag a tube along the bottom. It works real well in areas that are receiving a lot of fishing pressure, because the bass are seeing something different."

Klein drags deeper main lake structure — such as extensive points and ridges with distinct breaklines.

He fishes the tube on a 1/4-ounce darter-head jig with a plastic weedguard. In relatively shallow water, he switches to a Carolina rigged tube bait.

"The tube will draw strikes from suspended bass, and from bottom-hugging fish as deep as 40 to 50 feet," declares Klein.

BOUNCING WESTERN RIVERS

Tubes prove equally effective for a number of species, including smallmouth, which swim the West's great rivers. According to Chris Hendershot, rivers and streams are ideal settings for the versatile bait.

"When you stop to think about it," says the bait manufacturer, "fishing the bait in a river environment is probably the most productive way to fish a Gitzit, because you have all these tentacles moving with the current — all the time."

As one would expect, it's important to cast the bait upstream, allowing the current to push it naturally downstream. Casting upstream is also necessary to make the bait work close to the bottom, where, Hendershot says, it is most effective.

Current speed determines the amount of weight required to get the bait to the bottom. It's impor-

tant to use just enough weight to keep the bait moving along the bottom. Too little weight and the bait never makes it to the bottom; too much weight, and the bait snags in the rocky streambed.

For fishing relatively shallow or slow moving water, Hendershot recommends a 1/16-ounce jig. If the water is relatively deep or when casting against a stiff wind, try a 3/8-ounce darter-head jig.

Color selection for rivers and streams depends on water clarity and cloud cover, he advises. In clear water, anglers will want to use translucent smoke, shad and crawfish colors. Where crawfish are plentiful, popular colors among river anglers are green and green-with-shrimp.

A smaller bait, such as 1 1/2 or 2 1/2 inches, might be more appropriate for stream angling. But whatever size and weight, the tube is not meant to be a fast moving bait.

"Bass are not looking for something that's moving by them at 30 miles an hour," Hendershot says. "Usually, they're out scouring the bottom, looking for forage — like crawfish or sculpins. They want a slow, subtle presentation, and that's what the tube bait gives them."

TARGET BASS chasing larger shad in summer by positioning your boat in shallow water and casting out to the deeper water. This keeps the bait in front of the bass for the longest possible period.

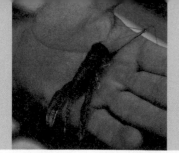

BASS FISHING WITH CRAWFISH CLONES

New plastic craws look good enough to eat

WHEN DION HIBDON MOLDED A PLASTIC CRAWFISH as a science project in 1978, he spawned a whole new generation of lures that took the bass fishing world by storm.

His father, Guido Hibdon, made the plastic craw famous by using it to win the 1980 and 1981 BASSMASTER Missouri Invitationals. The lure, dubbed the Guido Bug, was also instrumental in Hibdon's ascension to the pinnacle of professional bass fishing when he won the 1988 BASS Masters Classic and earned two consecutive B.A.S.S. Angler-of-the-Year titles in the early 1990s. The Hibdons' success with the Guido Bug led other lure manufacturers to flood the market with other realistic-looking craws.

While the plastic craw remained an effective lure throughout the 1990s, other soft plastics, such as tubes and creature-type baits, have gained more notoriety lately. The next generation of realistic craws, however, could change that trend.

Mad Man Lures initiated the latest crawfish craze with its Mad Man Crawfish, a three-dimensional plastic crawfish with a solid tail section, hollow body and realistic-looking pincers, legs and feelers that provide lifelike

(Opposite page) LOUISIANA ANGLER Sam Swett employs Yum Craw Bugs in a wide array of applications, ranging from flipping to buzzing on top. He finds craws to be especially attractive to big bass.

Plastic Crawfish

A number of manufacturers offer crawfish imitators. Crawfish tubes (far right) can be rigged Texas style on a wide gap worm hook, or outfitted with a jighead that is slipped inside the body cavity. Special jigs are also available for standard crawfish baits, which can be fished by flipping, Carolina rigging and a variety of other techniques.

The hollow bodies of realistic craws and craw tubes make the lures fall slowly, and they provide a realistic texture when bass bite down on the baits. The soft plastic material also enables easy hook penetration for better hook sets.

REALISTIC CRAWS are ideal for flipping in heavy cover, such as flooded bushes and surface-growing aquatic weeds. They can be rigged weedless on a wide gap worm hook.

action as it moves through the water. While the Guido Bug gained more notoriety during its prime, the Mad Man Crawfish has still influenced other lure companies to manufacture similar models of realistic crawfish. Joining the realistic craw movement are PRADCO, with its Yum Craw Bug; Lake Fork Trophy Bait & Tackle, with its Fork Craw; and Storm Lures, with its Rattle Hot Craw Tube.

"It's just one step more in the natural process," says Texas pro Kelly Jordon, who notes the Fork Craw has smaller pincers than the first generation of craws. "Bass are more likely to eat a crawfish that doesn't have big claws."

Oklahoma B.A.S.S. competitor Edwin Evers believes the Mad Man Crawfish Tube and Crawfish Worm have many more realistic features than the earlier plastic crawfish. "I'm presenting something to the fish that they have never seen before," he says. "The old craws were just a piece of plastic with two arms that stuck out; Mad Man has put eyes, tentacles and ribs on its crawfish."

The new craws can be used as jig trailers or Texas rigged baits similar to the old generation of lures. Evers occasionally uses a Mad Man Crawfish as a jig trailer, but most of the time he prefers the soft plastic as a stand-alone lure, especially in clear water, because of its lifelike appearance. "It looks more realistic than a jig, and has an added feature in that it gives off bubbles as it goes down," says Evers. In addition to the bubble action, the hollow body of this craw produces a slower fall than the earlier crawfish models.

The craw's design allows anglers to rig and present the soft plastic in a myriad of ways. CITGO BASSMASTER Tournament Trail competitors are using the next generation of craws for flipping, sight fishing, Carolina rigging, drop shotting and topwater tactics.

FLIPPING FAVORITE

While practicing for a tournament on the Potomac River in his first year on the circuit, Evers quickly discovered the effectiveness of the Mad Man Crawfish as a flipping bait. "The very first day I tied that thing on, it was absolutely phenomenal," he recalls. "I had 24 or 25 pounds in a heartbeat while flipping lily pads."

Evers prefers the 3-inch Mad Man Crawfish Tube for flipping as a jig trailer or Texas rigged with a 3/16- to 5/16-ounce sinker and a 2/0 offset hook. When using other sizes of the Mad Man Crawfish Tubes or Worms, he matches the baits with the following hooks: 2/0 or 3/0 extra-wide gap flipping hook for the 3 1/2-inch craw tube; 4/0 or 5/0 extra-wide gap for the 4-inch craw tube; 4/0 worm hook for the craw worm; and Gamakatsu G-Mag for the 5-inch craw tube.

When fishing clear water, Evers opts for Mad Man craws in green pumpkin. The Oklahoma pro favors junebug hues for stained conditions, black neon for murky water and black-and-blue craws for muddy water.

The craw tube also serves as an ideal trailer for swimming a jig in the fall. Evers selects a 3 1/2-inch Crawfish Tube in silver or white that he impales on a 3/8-ounce white jig. "It has a lot of flash when I'm swimming it," says Evers.

Fellow Oklahoma pro Marty Fourkiller discovered that Storm Lures' Rattle Hot Craw appealed to postspawn bass during a tournament on Lake Champlain. Fourkiller combined a brown-and-gold craw with a 3/8-ounce brown and pumpkin jig, which he flipped into swarms of bass fry. "The water was clear, so I could actually see the fry in the top of a bush," he recalls. "When I threw it in there, it scattered the fry, which were being protected by bass underneath."

After letting the jig-and-craw fall to the bottom, Fourkiller would jiggle it a couple of times and then swim it through the fry. The presentation produced several keepers for Fourkiller that day, as he finished with a limit weighing more than 14 pounds.

The longer pincers of the Storm Lures craw create more action on the back of a jig, Fourkiller believes. "You have to have something so when you pump that jig, the trailer will fluff or move like a real crawfish pincer," he advises.

CAROLINA RIG CRAWS

The Fork Craw has become one of Texas pro Kelly Jordon's favorite Carolina rig baits because of its realistic appearance and a hollow body that allows it to float off the bottom. "When it first came out, it was like using live bait," claims Jordon. "They ate it like it was the real deal."

Jordon enhances the sound and smell of his Carolina rig bait by stuffing rattles and cotton swabs dowsed with scent into the craw's cavity. Jordon believes another advantage of the hollow body is that it allows a hook to penetrate the plastic easier, which results in a better hook set for all presentations.

The Fork Craw can handle a big hook for flipping, but Jordon settles for a 3/0 offset, light wire worm hook for his Carolina rig tactics. For most situations, Jordon matches his Fork Craw with a 1-ounce sinker, since the heavier weight casts the bulky bait farther and creates more sound as it bangs along the bottom.

DROP SHOT DANDY

In early spring and later in the summer, B.A.S.S. veteran Rick Lillegard attaches a Yum Craw Bug to a drop shot rig to catch big smallmouth on Lake Winnipesaukee. "It's a bait that you can either drag or use vertically," says Lillegard.

The New Hampshire angler drags the lure in the early spring on a short drop (hook rigged above the sinker about 3 to 6 inches) when the submerged vegetation is close to the bottom. He

lengthens the drop and presents it vertically during the summer or in high-pressure situations any other time of the year when bass suspend.

The drop shot craw is especially effective for consistently working in the strike zone of big smallmouth. "I have heard from divers that a lot of the larger smallmouth will consistently suspend 3 to 4 feet off the bottom," says Lillegard.

A watermelon or green pumpkin Craw Bug works best for Lillegard's drop shot tactics on clear lakes. He also has caught fish on brown-and-orange or black-and-red craws while drop shotting on various waters throughout the country.

TOPWATER TRICKS

Buzzing a Yum Craw Bug over emergent grass and lily pads is one of Sam Swett's favorite ways to fish a realistic craw. The craw's hollow body keeps it buoyant and the pincers give it a flapping action on the surface, but the tail is the key to its topwater effectiveness. "The tail almost has like a reversed tip to help keep it sliding across the top of the water."

The Louisiana pro sticks the craw on a weighted, weedless hook. The weighted hook permits him to cast the craw farther, and the weedguard prevents grass from sticking on the hook as the lure glides across the weed mats. He employs a steady retrieve across the grass until it comes to an opening in the mat, then Swett lets the lure sink into the hole. As it descends, the lure flutters like a falling crawfish.

Besides looking more realistic, the next generation of craws is adapting into more versatile baits Bassmasters can depend on for a variety of tactics, from top to bottom.

REALISTIC CRAWS make especially good trailers for rubber legged jigs. Evers uses a silver flake Mad Man craw tube behind a white jig. He swims the jig-and-craw combo around weeds and similar cover in the fall.

HUMBLE FRENCH FRY GAINS NOTORIETY

This no-frills bait simply catches bass

IF BEAUTY CAN BE FOUND in simplicity alone, then the soft plastic genre of lures referred to as the "French fry" should be hanging under a display light on some museum wall. If the unattractive can somehow be enticing in its own peculiar way, then the French fry is truly the ugly duckling that has become bass fishing's belle of the ball.

At first glance, there is absolutely nothing special about the humble French fry.

have the crinkle-cut look of the fast-food side orders for which they are named.

In recent years, the French fry has emerged as one of the prime Carolina rigging lures of the top tournament pros. The plastic lizard is still the undisputed king of the dragging crowd, but the French fry has somehow wormed its way into the Carolina rig tackleboxes of the most knowledgeable competitors. As a result, nearly every soft plastics maker includes some version of the bait in its lineup — and that speaks volumes about the lure's effectiveness.

"In tournaments, the most important Carolina rig lures are a French fry-type lure and a lizard," praises Mark Davis, former B.A.S.S. Angler of the Year and a CITGO BASS Masters Classic champion. "Day in and day out, you're going to catch more fish on those two than on any other lure."

It catches big bass as well.

In a B.A.S.S. event on Texas' Rayburn Reservoir, North Carolina pro Jerry Rhyne opened his competitors' eyes to the power of a French fry with a 31-pound, five bass limit caught on a 4-inch Zoom Centipede. Included were trophy fish weighing 11 pounds, 9 ounces, and 10 pounds, 8 ounces.

Those results did not surprise Rhyne, who points out that today's French fry is a descendant of the "Do Nothing" style of baits that anglers have been fishing in the Carolinas since he was a youngster.

AN ALLURING QUESTION

The pros who swear by the French fry's allure are at a loss for words to explain its appeal.

"Why does it work? 'Why' is always the hardest question in this sport," admits Ken Cook, a former Classic champion and

No high-tech computer-aided design. No flashy qualities. No lifelike action. No alluring appendages. Nothing that would make the uneducated angler pluck it from a tackle store shelf.

Except that it has a proven track record for catching bass — including some giants.

In case you haven't been introduced, the French fry is a short, squatty, box-cut piece of plastic. Most are 4 to 5 inches long and

ALTHOUGH CAROLINA rigging is the most popular method of fishing French fries, Texas rigging the bait can produce similar results.

Ken Cook's Two Lure Carolina Rig

Former Classic champion Ken Cook had grown frustrated with the aggressive bass that actually struck the large weight of his Carolina rig instead of the attractive soft plastic creature swimming behind it. His solution not only solved that problem, but also enabled him to catch many doubles in several tournaments.

The Oklahoma pro devised a two hook rig that enables him to fish both a French fry and a lizard. And bass no longer bite his sinker.

Cook's Carolina rig begins with about 3 feet of 10- to 20-pound mono leader. At the top is a 1/2- to 1-ounce brass weight followed by two glass beads. The main line is tied to a three-way swivel that allows him to create two leaders. At the end of the main leader is a 6-inch lizard impaled on a 3/0 hook. To catch the bass that attack the weight, Cook affixes a 1 1/2- to 2-inch leader of 25-pound test to the other arm of the swivel. At the end of this tiny leader is a 1/0 hook Texas rigged with a 4-inch French fry.

"You would be surprised how often the short leader just below the sinker catches fish," Cook says. "It's not unusual to catch two at a time on this rig."

fisheries biologist. "There is no answer as to why. We don't know why a bass does the things it does. The French fry must have a certain flutter as it goes down — more of a lifelike sink than we realize — reminiscent of some sort of dying animal. It doesn't have the wiggles and 'be-bops' and all that.

"Fish don't think. Bass don't run around thinking that a French fry doesn't look like anything it would eat. So I think it is partly a curiosity thing. They don't have any way to find out what it is except to put it in their mouths."

SOME FRENCH FRY BAITS are more buoyant than others. Once you figure out how the bass are relating to the bottom, select the leader length and French fry that will keep the bait hovering in the strike zone.

Davis adds, "If you notice, most minnows just dart around. They swim real straight. And I think that is what a 4-inch French fry-style worm imitates."

Four time Classic qualifier Bernie Schultz emphasizes that its small stature and texture are the French fry's main attributes. Bass tend to hold on to these baits for a longer period of time than other plastic creatures, in his opinion.

SEASONS AND SITUATIONS

Despite their inability to explain the charm of the French fry, the pros have definite thoughts on when and where these lures produce best.

With the exception of the coldest portions of winter, Texas pro Bruce Benedict relies on his Jawtec French Fry throughout the year. It begins with prespawn fishing around secondary points with sparse cover (the same situation later applies to postspawners).

He also drags the lure along shallow spawning flats. In summer, the French fry is back where it belongs — in deep water. Benedict has discovered that it is especially productive when fished along submerged roadbeds, ledges and dropoffs. In the fall, the Texas pro uses the French fry to cover a variety of depths and structure, including creek channels, ditches and shallow flats.

It was early spring on Rayburn when Jerry Rhyne and his Zoom Centipede produced his impressive catch. Rhyne targeted a 20-foot ditch that merges with an old pond dam about 8 feet below the surface. He caught the largest stringer of his career by methodically pulling the 4-inch Centipede along the top of the rock dam.

For Oklahoma pro O.T. Fears, the French fry is most productive during the pre and postspawn phases, as well as in clear water — situations where its compact profile is especially attractive.

"A French fry seems to work better after the sun comes up and the day gets brighter. That's because it's a smaller bait," he interjects. "A lizard might be better early, before the sun gets up. But by, say, 10 o'clock, you get fewer and fewer bites on a lizard. That's when I go to a French fry."

A French fry is a surprisingly good search lure for pro Kevin VanDam.

"I like to get on edges like an inside grassline or outside grassline or points," he explains. "I work the lure fairly quickly, which is not possible with other lures, like a spinnerbait, in deep water."

The experts seem to agree that the French fry is most valuable on days when conditions are less than favorable and the fishing is difficult.

"A French fry is a finesse option for the Carolina rig," Schultz says. "It's great for real lethargic bass, such as just after a front or on a heavily pressured lake. When the fish are off, for whatever reason, and you can't get them to take Carolina rigged lizards or Texas rigged soft plastics, the French fry is a really good way to get some strikes.

"It's probably the tube jig of Carolina rigs."

RETRIEVAL AND RIGGING

This is one bait of which the driver must take control. The French fry has no design features to draw attention to itself. It has to be *worked*.

The French fry is fished no differently than other Carolina rig choices. With the rod tip low to the water, the lure is pulled across the bottom with the typical horizontal sweeping motion. Any slack line is then reeled in and the movement is repeated. VanDam occasionally "pops" the bait along the bottom, while Benedict prefers to drag and pause the lure frequently.

As with all Carolina rig plastics, it is important to allow the heavy weight above the leader to maintain contact with the lake floor throughout the retrieve. The sinker dredges up silt and mud, which often attracts curious bass.

"When I feel a strike with a bait like the French fry, I let the fish pull the line or rod tip down before I set the hook," Schultz advises. "I want to figure out what direction the fish is traveling and set against that direction."

With the French fry, the rigging details are usually similar to those used for other Carolina rig offerings: a 3/4- or 1-ounce weight; plastic or glass bead (to protect the knot from the sinker and to make noise); barrel swivel; a 2- to 3-foot leader of 12- to 17-pound-test line; and a 2/0 to 3/0 hook.

In certain situations, Schultz substitutes one or two split shot — positioned 18 to 24 inches above the French fry — for the conventional Carolina rig. For example, he split shots when smallmouth fishing in northern lakes like Lake Ontario; when fishing deep, ultraclear waters of the Southwest; and when working shallow, clear spawning flats on Lake Okeechobee.

"Believe it or not, I sometimes fish a (Texas rig) French fry with a hook and no weight," VanDam states. "I just twitch it around like you would a Slug-Go. And it catches fish that way."

The French fry may be the most uninspiring bass lure of all, but its mysterious allure has prompted the pros to develop some highly imaginative methods of exploiting its fish catching abilities.

AMAZINGLY, even huge bass will hit finesse-size French fries.

NEW TRICKS FOR SPIDER GRUBS

There are a lot of reasons to add this bait to your go-to list

BOUNCING spider jigs along rocky banks is a super tactic for catching crawfish-hungry smallmouth.

REMARKABLY, the spider grub is not a staple in everyone's tacklebox. But it's a long time favorite of West Coast anglers, becoming more popular with smallmouth anglers in the Northeast and might be the hottest soft plastic lure in the Great Lakes region.

The spider jig — Yamamoto's Hula Grub is probably the best-known example — is made of soft plastic with either single or double curled tails.

It has a spider-legs collar or skirt on the head, which sets it apart from traditional grubs. Most anglers thread these 2- to 5-inch baits on jigheads, although they can be rigged Texas style on worm hooks.

Depending upon how you fish it, the grub looks deceptively like a darting crawfish. It is most effective in clear water. Initially, it was designed for finessing down rocky walls of clear canyon lakes or crawling along deep, rocky flats. But as anglers

have discovered, it can be effective in a wider variety of situations.

The lure is compact like a jig-and-pig, as versatile as a worm, can be fished vertically or horizontally, and fast or slow. You can pitch it, flip it, swim it, hop it or drag it on the bottom. A finesse lure? Yes, but one with a lot of options. Here are ways some of the experts use it:

A SEARCH TOOL

Northern anglers use spider jigs to cover water quickly when they suspect largemouth and smallmouth are feeding on crawfish around scattered patches of weeds and rocks on shallow flats.

"I used to fish jigs with pork frogs in those situations, but the spider jig works better in clear water," says Greg Mangus, a South Bend, Ind., angler. "You can fish it faster than the jig, cover water quickly and trigger more reaction strikes."

He believes the translucent colors available in spider jigs make them more effective in clear water than do standard jigs.

Mangus fishes the spider jig horizontally in an erratic, jerkbait-type motion. The lure is constantly moving, yet kept on or near the bottom so it looks like a crawfish scooting madly along the bottom.

When fishing open flats with scattered grass, Mangus rigs the grub on a jighead. If the cover is thick, he uses a brushguard, or it can be rigged Texas style as well.

"You'll land more fish if the hook is exposed, and where we're fishing it, there's little concern

WHEN FISHING spider jigs, target shallow flats next to deep water. If rock and vegetation are nearby, all the better.

Shopping For Spider Jigs

Trying to choose the right hula grub can be a confusing proposition. While they may all look similar, there are subtle differences that can affect your fishing success.

For example, says pro Ken McIntosh, some manufacturers' plastics aren't as soft, have thicker legs and won't work as well in cold water or with light jigheads.

"Rig the bait and drop it over the side of the boat," suggests McIntosh. "If the legs don't vibrate on the fall, you're probably not going to catch as many fish."

McIntosh recommends anglers use the lightest jighead possible. But in water deeper than 10 feet, a heavier jig may be necessary.

"When a lightweight lure falls in deep water, the line drag can inhibit the action of the legs and take it longer to get to the bottom," he offers. "It's also more difficult to feel the bait with light jigs in deep water."

Browns and greens are best performers in the North, while shad and crawfish colors tend to work better in the South. In stained waters, opaque colors can be more effective. Most anglers prefer double tails, although the single tails can be productive when swimming the bait to imitate a shad.

McIntosh also favors salted or flavor-enhanced spider jigs because bass seem to bite and hold them better.

WHEN MATCHED with the appropriate colors, spider grubs closely resemble crawfish.

TO MAKE the hula grub look like a crawfish scooting along the bottom, Greg Mangus pulls the rod sideways in a rhythmic jerking motion. He pulls until he feels the weight of the bait, drops slack in the line, then repeats the action. These short, rapid movements keep the bait moving without jerking it far off the bottom.

about snagging," he explains. "Actually, I like for the grub hook to catch a little bit of weed, because I can pop it free and trigger a strike that way."

He opts for 3/16- or 1/4-ounce jigheads, depending upon the water depth, wind, current or how difficult it is to keep the lure on bottom. He fishes them on a soft, 7-foot graphite spinning outfit. He prefers 8-pound line, but will switch to 6 or 10, depending upon the density of the cover.

Working the bait properly takes practice. Essentially, you want it scooting in short bursts along the bottom without making excessive hops. Pull it too hard or vertically and you lose contact with the bottom. Keep the rod low to the water and to the side of the boat, diminishing the effect wind may have blowing against the line.

Mangus pulls the rod tip in short, rapid movements, applying enough pressure to feel the weight of the bait, then drops the rod tip back toward the lure. Each time he moves the rod, the bait scoots 6 inches to a foot at a time. The reel is used only to take up excess slack.

"Pay close attention to what the weight of your jig feels like while you're working it," he says. "You won't feel many of the strikes, but the bait will feel mushy, heavy, or perhaps there will be no weight at all. That's when I sweep the rod, put a bend in it and keep reeling. If it's a weed, it pops off. If it's a fish, you've got him."

OTHER TECHNIQUES

Swimming the grub — B.A.S.S. pro Kim Stricker recalls how a change from a jerkbait to a spider grub helped him in a Michigan tournament.

"I was fishing patchy weeds in 5 feet of water," says Stricker. "The bass stopped hitting, but they continued to follow the jerkbait. I switched to a cinnamon-color Yamamoto Hula Grub and reeled it erratically over patchy weeds, occasionally stopping it. The changing speeds got them biting again, and I won the tournament."

The drag — Missouri pro Jeff Fletcher uses a slow dragging technique when fishing spiders on long gravel points of Missouri's deep, clear lakes. He rigs the lure on a stand-up jig and pulls it slowly over the rocky bottom.

"There are always crawfish on those points and the smallmouths and Kentucky bass will hang around there year-round," he explains. "I prefer to work it extremely slow to ensure it stays on the bottom."

Working the bluffs — Jay Yelas may hail from Texas, but he learned to fish in the West. The spider grub rigged on a 1/2-ounce (or heavier) football jighead was one of his favorites for fishing shady pockets of steep bluffs.

"You can cover a lot of water by simply getting tight to the walls and throwing the jig into the shade," he describes. "I'd let it hit bottom, hop it a couple of times, then reel it in and hit another spot. It's ideal when looking for aggressive fish and covering deep water quickly."

Carolina rigging — Pro Ken McIntosh uses the grub on Carolina rigs in deep water. However, he adds a 1/32-ounce Gambler screw-in sinker to the head of the bait in addition to the heavy sliding sinker on the main line.

"The only purpose of the screw-in sinker is to prevent the plastic bait from sliding down the 3/0 hook," he explains. "I skin-hook the spider grub to keep it weedless, and rarely miss a strike. When I feel the heavy sinker pulling into rocks or heavy cover, I shake the line to make the spider grub dance. That's when most strikes occur."

Suspended fish — Lake Fork guide and pro Stan Gerzsenyi says a Yamamoto Hula Grub can save the day when cold fronts have bass suspended over structure. He rigs it Texas style on the rods of customers who are unfamiliar with more specialized bass fishing techniques. He says it's easier for them to fish and detect strikes.

"I've had customers outfish me on tough days when I'm fishing a crankbait or spinnerbait," he explains. "When bass are suspended, I use a small weight or no weight at all and let it flutter down

NORTHERN ANGLER Greg Mangus likes the versatility of spider jigs. To fool a largemouth into biting, he will fish it vertically, horizontally, pitch it, flip it, hop it, Carolina rig it, and drag it along the lake bottom.

slowly, shaking it occasionally. By keeping the bait in front of the suspended fish longer, they're more apt to bite that than something falling rapidly past them."

Get the picture? Spider jigs are extremely versatile and nearly foolproof. If you're looking for strikes when fishing is tough, this is one lure that can save the day.

Rigging Options

Most pros favor rigging the spider grub on a leadhead jig when fishing rocky areas. The shape of the leadhead will make the bait stand in different positions on the lake bottom, and anglers should experiment to find which one bass prefer. When fishing vegetation, Texas rig the bait and experiment with different weight sizes. Start with a 1/8-ounce weight, so the bait falls slowly, giving bass time to strike. Move up to a 1/2-ounce weight if looking for the reaction strike.

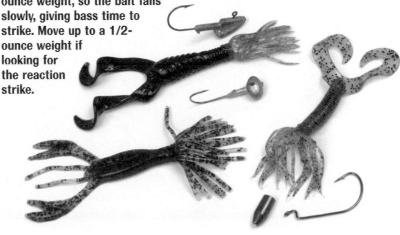

HARD BAITS

Angling for a bigger bite?
Switch to jigs,
spinnerbaits and other
hard headed lures . . .

GET A PH.D. IN SPINNERBAITING

Advanced tactics for an elementary bait

(Opposite page) BIG BASS like big meals, and spinnerbaits with multiple blades offer a buffet to hungry largemouth.

SOME LURES REQUIRE a fair degree of skill to fish properly — jigs, plastic worms and jerkbaits come to mind. But a spinnerbait is virtually idiot-proof. Even the rankest amateur can chunk it out, reel it in and, sooner or later, catch a bass on it.

Spinnerbaits have been among the most popular bass lures for decades, and I've written dozens of articles about how, when and where to fish 'em. But it wasn't until researching this feature that I realized how little I really knew about these popular lures. As I discovered, there's spinnerbait fishin', and then there's *spinnerbait* fishin'. You're about to receive a Ph.D.-level education in spinnerbaitin' from one of this lure's premier tacticians. If your success with spinnerbaits doesn't escalate dramatically after reading what follows, you probably weren't paying attention in class.

ANATOMY OF A SPINNERBAIT

Cleveland, Ohio, pro Frank Scalish quickly has gained the respect of his peers as a highly proficient spinnerbait fisherman.

"Spinnerbaits are easily the most versatile lures in your tacklebox," says Scalish. "By altering their various components, you can make them perform exactly the right way in any situation."

Weight selection should be totally situational, he continues. "I know fishermen who won't throw anything but a 3/8-ounce spinnerbait because they saw some pro using one on television. It's far better to select the lure weight according to conditions."

He likes a 1/4-ounce spinnerbait when fishing wood cover in stained water less than 2 feet deep, and he seldom throws a 3/8 ounce, which

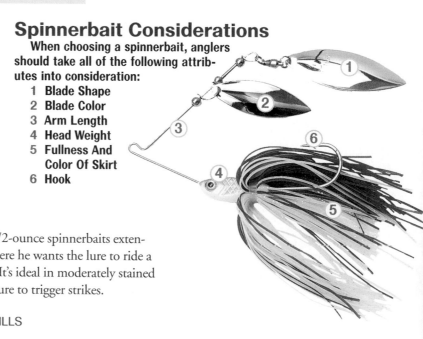

Spinnerbait Considerations

When choosing a spinnerbait, anglers should take all of the following attributes into consideration:

1 Blade Shape
2 Blade Color
3 Arm Length
4 Head Weight
5 Fullness And Color Of Skirt
6 Hook

is the gold standard for most anglers. Instead, he uses 1/2-ounce spinnerbaits extensively; this is a highly versatile weight that works anywhere he wants the lure to ride a little lower — but not *too* low — in the water column. It's ideal in moderately stained to clear water, and it can be fished faster than a lighter lure to trigger strikes.

The Time-Tested In-Line Spinner

The words, "in-line spinners," just seem to bring out the boy in some men.

"I've fished with in-line spinners since I was a little kid," says Shaw Grigsby, a perennial CITGO BASS Masters Classic qualifier from Florida. "That was the bait my dad used to get me hooked on fishing for rainbow trout up in the mountains. I learned real early that you can catch everything on it — bass, crappie, walleye, trout. That's the neat thing about these baits."

"I was raised in northern California, where I was introduced to fishing in-line spinners for trout," adds Gary Klein, who went on to win two B.A.S.S. Angler-of-the-Year titles. "During my trout fishing experience, I also caught a lot of bass on them — including some phenomenal largemouth and smallmouth. That got me hooked on in-line spinners."

The in-line spinner ushered most of us into the wonderful world of fishing. Its ability to attract fish of all types ensured that our introduction was a satisfying one.

No other lure catches such a variety of species, including almost everything that swims in fresh water. That is particularly true of the major bass species (largemouth, smallmouth and spotted).

Even today's in-line spinners are born of the simple design of yesteryear. Components consist, basically, of a revolving blade pinned to the top of a straight wire shaft — a streamlined package that is easy to cast and provides the slim profile, vibration and light reflection of a live baitfish.

APPLICATIONS AND STRATEGIES

Without doubt, the typical stream setting — moving water with current breaks and small eddy pockets — is where the in-line spinner is most productive, particularly when it is retrieved in a natural, downcurrent manner. But these lures are by no means limited to flowing water.

"With in-line spinners, the first consideration is that they are not weedless," Klein says. "That's why it is not usually a good choice for largemouth in cover. With this lure, I have a tendency to stop my cast short or throw wide. I miss targets by messing with the cast because I'm worried about getting hung up all of the time.

"I usually fish it in clear water for smallmouth or spotted bass that are in open water around shell, clay and rock. Lake Lanier is good for fishing them. I also fish them more for deep, suspended fish or if I'm just going down an open shoreline."

Underwater rocks and wood are Grigsby's favorite places to cast an in-line spinner. The lure also is among his top choices in summer when bass are positioned underneath boat docks and overhanging tree limbs.

"You can sling an in-line spinner well back under a dock, because it casts like a bullet," he explains. "Because of their size, they're less likely to get hung up. Even though they have an open treble hook, you usually can just reel them back from under a dock without much problem. And an in-line spinner hovers near the surface, so you can bring it across brushpiles and around all kinds of neat stuff where you find bass holding in the summertime."

UNDERSTANDING HOW the components of a spinnerbait affect its action will guarantee more bass, says Frank Scalish.

Scalish's secret weapon is a 3/4-ounce spinnerbait. "This is my favorite weight in clear smallmouth lakes like St. Clair and Erie. Here, smallies often suspend in the 'twilight zone' — the depth where you can just barely see a spinnerbait's blades flashing," he explains. "A 3/4-ounce lure gets into that depth range quickly, and stays there. I also use a 3/4 ounce in real windy conditions, and in heavy current."

Blade shape, he says, is another factor worth considering.

Colorado — "This rounded, heavily cupped blade style creates maximum vibration and minimum flash, making it your best choice in muddy water, where bass feel it rather than see it. In stained water, where there is some visibility, I like silver or copper blades — spray copper blades with clear lacquer to minimize tarnish. Colorado blades are also good for fishing structures with a rapid slope into deep water, because they spin nicely when dropping."

Willowleaf — "This popular blade style has

THE POSITION of your rod tip can affect the depth of your spinnerbait by several feet. When a bass hits, remember the location of your rod tip, the speed you were reeling and the cadence of your presentation, then duplicate it.

lots of flash and little vibration; use it in clear water. The long, slender shape comes through grass better than other styles. Willowleaf blades resemble baitfish; a tandem willowleaf with both blades the same color mimics a large baitfish like a full-grown gizzard shad, while a tandem willowleaf with one silver and one gold blade looks more like a school of smaller baitfish. Willowleaf blades are easy to 'burn' (retrieve very quickly)."

Indiana or Oklahoma — "These teardrop- or turtle-shell-shape blades are a compromise between the rounded Colorado and the elongated willowleaf. I like this style in water with 1 to 2 feet of visibility; it gives a good combination of thump and flash."

Along with blade shape, blade size is yet another factor that dramatically affects a spinnerbait's performance. "In murky to muddy water, run a big Colorado blade on a lightweight spinnerbait," Scalish notes. "You can c-r-a-w-l this combination across logs and stumps, or you can reel it fast just under the surface so the blade makes a wake. When fishing deep, clear water, I like the opposite setup — a small Colorado blade on a heavier lure."

Small blades create less drag, Scalish points out. "They're better in current, and any other time you're fishing fast. I also like small blades in extremely clear water, where a big blade with maximum flash can spook bass. In stained water, where you want a good balance of flash and vibration, try a Colorado in front and a willowleaf in the back."

Painted blades play a role in Scalish's game plan as well. "Painted blades don't flash like plated blades," he notes. "Instead, they 'strobe' — like the blue light on a police car. I like painted blades in rainy or overcast conditions, when there's less light to reflect off a plated blade. Smallmouth have this thing about chartreuse blades retrieved overhead; in clear lakes, they'll swim up 30 feet to chase them. A spinnerbait with chartreuse blades and an orange skirt fished close to weedy banks is a killer largemouth lure; it resembles a bluegill."

Sweat The Small Stuff

Bass may be eating spinnerbaits for a variety of reasons, color being just one. A subtle difference between baits could be key: Are the blades hammered, making the flash more subdued? Is there a spot near the head, making the bait more closely resemble shad? Is the willowleaf blade sharply angled, making the blade spin at a higher rate of speed, giving the flash a different rhythm?

The gauge (thickness) of the wire used in the frame also has a bearing on the lure's performance. "Standard stainless steel wire varies in thickness from one lure manufacturer to the next," Scalish says. "With steel, the thinner the wire, the more vibration the blades will emit. But the trade-off is an increased likelihood that the frame will break or get out of tune. Titanium wire allows you to use a spinnerbait with a thin frame for more vibration, without sacrificing durability or alignment precision."

Most Bassmasters are familiar with "short-arm" and "long-arm" spinnerbaits. "This refers to the length of the wire on which the blades are mounted," Scalish explains.

"Short-arm spinnerbaits are best in vertical situations, as when fishing bluff banks. The short length of wire over the hook allows the blade to 'helicopter' (spin freely) when the lure drops straight down. Long-arm spinnerbaits are better for horizontal presentations, and anytime you

ROLAND MARTIN has a doctorate in spinnerbaiting, using the bait on the way to many of his 19 B.A.S.S. victories.

want a fast retrieve. A short-arm lure tends to roll over when you burn it."

CHASING SKIRTS

The skirt is yet another critical spinnerbait component. "Most skirts today are made of silicone, a synthetic material," Scalish says. "Living rubber skirts were used for years, and are still favored by some for their fluid action. Synthetic skirts won't melt, and are less prone to stick together. They can also be produced in translucent colors, which are highly effective in clear water."

Scalish prefers Terminator Quick-Change skirts, which are composed of thin, square and flat rectangular silicone strands.

"This combination causes the skirt to undulate and pulse when the lure is retrieved," he says. "I modify my skirts a bit by turning the spinnerbait upside down and trimming all the square-shaped strands shorter than the rectangular strands. This makes the skirt billow out more, especially on a stop-and-go retrieve. Skirt bulk is also an important factor to consider. In clear water, you want less bulk; I pluck every other strand from the skirt to thin it out. In murky water, a bulkier skirt is easier for the bass to see."

How about skirt color? "If you look at a shad swimming in clear water, notice that you can almost see through it," Scalish says. "Likewise, a translucent skirt is more realistic when visibility is high. In the clearest conditions, my favorite skirt colors are blue shad and speckled trout. A great

Trailer Trash?

Many pros don't use trailers on spinnerbaits because they believe them unnecessary. Others never throw a spinnerbait without some form of trailer. A good compromise: When power fishing, don't worry about using a trailer. When slow rolling or vertically presenting spinnerbaits, use one to help add action to the lure's descent.

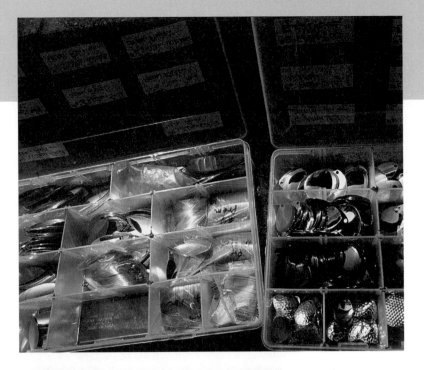

but highly overlooked color in clear water is golden shiner. All of these are translucent, yet slightly reflective, which creates a very subtle presentation."

Altering the skirt can turn short strikes into hookups, Scalish emphasizes. "If bass are nipping the bait, they're obviously attracted to it, so rather than change skirt color, I'll reduce its size by either plucking out strands or trimming the skirt with scissors. I leave the longest strands intact, so they feather out nicely behind the hook.

"If that doesn't work, *then* I'll switch colors, always making any changes in increments. For example, if they're bumping a lure with a white skirt, I may switch to a white-and-green skirt."

BRINGING IT HOME

Having the perfect spinnerbait for the job is one thing; retrieving it correctly is something else.

"The most misunderstood retrieve is *slow rolling,*" Scalish says. "Most anglers use this term to describe any slow, steady retrieve; but with a true slow roll, the lure touches bottom as much as possible without hanging up or losing blade action. Slow rolling is a retrieve intended for cold fronts and cold water, when bass are tight to bottom. It works best with a 1/2- to 3/4-ounce spinnerbait."

Moving the lure horizontally through the water column at normal spinnerbait speed is what Scalish refers to as a *slow retrieve.* "I use this retrieve when working submerged brush, stumps and weed edges. Here, the object is to fish the lure just deep enough so you can barely see the blades flashing."

Use an *intermittent* (stop and go) retrieve when you see bass following, but not striking, the lure. "With the rod tip at 11 o'clock, reel, stop abruptly so the lure drops on tight line like a pendulum for several feet, then start reeling again. Or, hold the rod at 10 o'clock, then snap it quickly to 11 o'clock to make the lure dart. One or the other action should trigger following fish to strike."

EVERYONE HAS his or her favorite go-to spinnerbait. To make this confidence lure more versatile, think about swapping out blades to match conditions.

THE SERIOUS spinnerbaiter carries a supply of spare spinnerbait components on board.

Burning the spinnerbait is a deadly tactic relatively few anglers outside the pro tour routinely employ. "A fast retrieve is awesome in clear water. Here, you're going for reaction strikes from curious fish. Make a long cast past a rockpile or ledge, and use a fast, steady retrieve, running the lure a foot or so under the surface. Sometimes entire schools of smallmouth will charge it."

NEW WRINKLES IN SPOONIN'

Deep holding bass are heavy metal fans

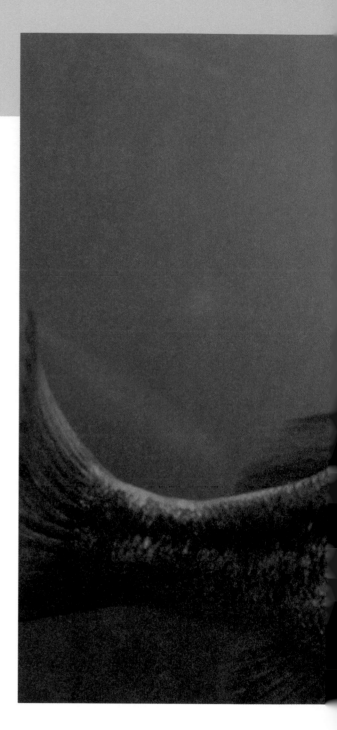

I F ANY BASS LURE has been miscast as one-dimensional, it's the jigging spoon. Its name says it all — or so most Bassmasters think. Ask most anglers who have used the bait, and they'll tell you a spoon is for vertical jigging, period.

The spoon has spent decades in the bottom of the average bass angler's tacklebox. It lacks the throbbing action of a crankbait, the enticing gurgle of a topwater lure, the spongy feel of a soft plastic crawfish. Most don't even cast out a spoon and reel it in, the way pike and trout anglers use the lures. Instead, they just toss it overboard, bump it up and down a few times and hope something big, mean and slimy hits it.

UNUSED AND UNAPPRECIATED

"Bassmasters are more aware of spoons now than in the past, but they're still underutilizing them," believes Tom Seward of Luhr-Jensen, one of the leading producers of fishing spoons.

BASS ANGLERS traditionally use spoons only for vertical jigging, but new spoons — and new ways of fishing them — are broadening the horizons of these metal lures.

Seward, a lure designer and expert multispecies angler, feels the spoon can be the deadliest lure in your tacklebox — if you don't leave it there.

"Spoons have been pigeonholed as vertical lures," Seward says. "Because most bass fishermen vertical-jig only in winter or midsummer, they forget about these lures the rest of the year. You can do a lot more with spoons than fish them straight up and down."

Just as the different designs of crankbaits, topwaters and soft plastic lures permit each to achieve different actions, different spoon designs produce different results.

"Most anglers feel a spoon is a spoon, but if you drop 10 different spoons in the water, you'll see 10 different actions," Seward notes. "Some spoons, such as our Crippled Herring, have what I call a 'falling leaf' action; others flutter like a dying baitfish; still others, especially slab spoons, drop like a rock. Some spoons work better than others in deep water.

"Flat, narrow spoons, which are thicker at one end than the other, are the most widely used by bass anglers, but their spiraling action makes them line-twisters."

Seward has found that on a given day, one spoon will consistently outperform all others in your tacklebox. "The problem is, you may not know which one is the hot one," he says. "That's why I always have several types of spoons handy, and I keep changing lures until I find the one with the profile or action bass want in the conditions I'm fishing."

Most Bassmasters use shiny metal spoons, but some more recent designs are startlingly realistic. The Crippled Herring, a slender, single-hook model, doesn't merely suggest a baitfish — it's the spittin' image of the real thing.

Painted spoons are usually snubbed by bass fishermen who think a spoon has to flash, but on overcast days, all metallic-finish lures tend to lose their flash, Seward notes. A painted spoon, like white or chartreuse, might draw more strikes in cloudy weather.

TO DEEP water bass, no other lure matches the tantalizing flutter of a dying baitfish as closely as a metal jigging spoon.

TO "CRACK" A SPOON, cast, let the spoon drop, then crack the rod tip upward sharply, causing the spoon to hop violently.

IN THE BOUNCE RETRIEVE, cast, let the spoon fall and pop the rod tip back to hop the spoon. Lower the rod tip slightly as spoon falls back.

FOR SCHOOLING BASS, cast past the fish, engaging the reel before the lure hits the water. Reel quickly to skip the spoon across the surface, then stop and let it drop into the school.

SPOONIN' TACKLE

Few anglers are more adept at milking maximum productivity from a spoon than Seward. He offers some tips to add new dimensions to the lure's utility.

"First, choose the right rod for spooning," he suggests. "Most spoon techniques are highly wrist-intensive. For this reason, a long, heavy rod can prove very fatiguing. I like a 5 1/2- to 6-foot medium heavy graphite baitcasting stick, one that's light, sensitive, powerful and easy to fish with all day."

The line you choose for spoon fishing can be vital to your success with this lure in more ways than one. "Unless the water is extremely clear, I'll use 20-pound mono with a spoon," Seward says. "Most spoon fishermen would choose line this heavy only when fishing around submerged trees or thick brush, where line abrasion is likely. But abrasion resistance isn't the only reason I like heavy line."

Large-diameter mono gives the spoon a slow rate of fall, Seward points out. "The lure's drop rate is the most important, and most ignored, factor in spoon fishing. How fast or slow it falls can determine whether or not your spoon will get eaten by a bass."

There are times when a fast drop rate is preferred, such as when bass are holding tight to a 35-foot ledge. "But most of the time, you want the spoon to fall slowly, like a dying baitfish," he says. "If it drops too fast, it usually won't get hit."

Many anglers are finding braided lines ideal for spoon fishing because of their tremendous strength and sensitivity. "But if you use one of these products, don't downsize your line diameter," Seward warns. "Twenty-pound braided line will make your spoon fall too quickly, because its diameter is so small. If you use braided line, make it 80 pound — not because you need all that strength, but because 80-pound braided line is the same diameter as 20-pound mono, resulting in a realistic drop rate."

There's another reason to use heavy line when

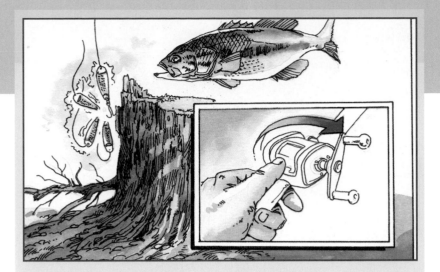

IF THE SPOON HANGS ON A STUMP, shake the rod tip so the spoon taps the stump. The noise attracts bass. Keep shaking until the lure is dislodged, then roll the wrist sideways so the spoon will flutter down.

spoonin'. This isn't just a numbers game. "Spoons are big fish lures," Seward declares. "You wouldn't believe the pictures of the big largemouth and smallmouth our customers send us, fish they caught on our various spoon designs. That's why it's critical to constantly check your line for abrasion, and retie as necessary."

Just as bass fishermen use line that is too thin, they also often use spoons that are too light for effective structure probing, Seward has found. "If your spoon isn't getting down to business, or if you lose touch with it, you're wasting your time. Go with a spoon that provides good bottom contact without sacrificing realism. A good starting weight is 3/4 ounce."

PRACTICE DIVERSITY

The spoon is a great lure for fishing all types of structures and bottom conditions, Seward has found — if you don't limit your presentation to vertical jigging.

"By varying your presentation, you can effectively fish a spoon in a broad range of situations, " he says. "My favorite way to fish a spoon is to make a long cast and bounce the lure back to the boat, somewhat like you'd fish a metal blade bait," he explains. "I'll cast it out and hop it back in 2- to 3-foot sweeps."

Each time the spoon drops, Seward lowers his rod tip just ahead of the lure's drop rate, so the spoon doesn't fall on a tight line. "Keeping just a little slack in the line allows the spoon to flutter straight down and not 'pendulum' toward you. When you see the line hop, set the hook — a bass has inhaled the bait," he says.

The spoon is often thought of as being nearly 100 percent wind resistant, but Seward knows a stiff breeze can dramatically affect the lure's drop rate. When the wind puts a big bow in your line, which often happens with heavy mono or braided products, the lure's rate of fall may be too slow. So, on windy days, compensate with smaller-diameter line.

"Cracking" a spoon injects a bass-enticing punch to your presentation. "This technique works best with a rounded spoon rather than a flat one," Seward explains. "Cast out, let the spoon fall to the bottom, then crack your rod tip, as though you were using it to throw a stone. This gives the spoon a violent hop and really excites fish. If there's a school of bass in the area, it'll pull them in for a look."

Seward likes vertical jigging as well, but throws some innovative twists into this technique.

"When jigging wood cover, sooner or later you'll hang up the spoon. If you play your cards right, you can pick up a bonus bass by taking a moment to try to shake the lure free, rather than immediately starting to jerk and pull.

"Gently shaking the rod tip causes the 'hung' spoon to tap against the cover, and a bass might be attracted by the noise and flash. Then when the spoon finally pops free, the bass is right there to grab it.

"I can't tell you how many fish I've caught immediately after the spoon popped loose from a stump," he says. "Once I figured out what was going on, I learned to pivot my wrist to one side as soon as the spoon worked loose. This lets it flutter back down naturally into the fish's face."

JIGGING SPOONS bear a strong resemblance in profile and flash to preferred bass forage, like this threadfin shad.

FOUR SEASONS OF JIGS
Jigs aren't just coldwater baits

NO SERIOUS BASS FISHERMAN would ever want to be without a jig. No other lure has retained such a regal reputation over the years. Today's high-tech baits may be pushing other traditional lures into the dark corners of America's tackleboxes, but the jig remains top drawer.

Why? Because veteran and novice anglers alike know that there's not a better big bass producer. And as more and more anglers are discovering, it's one of the most versatile lures available today.

That's quite a change from 15 years ago, when the jig was stereotyped as a lure for catching lethargic bass in cold water or from heavy cover.

"Big bass prefer crawfish over all types of forage, and the jig represents a crawfish better than any other lure," says pro Ken McIntosh of Indiana. "And because crawfish are prominent in most lakes year-round, the jig is capable of producing quality bites anytime, anywhere."

That philosophy is shared by most pros who wouldn't consider fishing a tournament without having at least one jig rod rigged and ready.

"Many anglers begin with other lures, and

when those aren't producing, they try the jig," says Arkansas pro Ron Shuffield. "The jig is my first choice, regardless of the season. I know that if the bass are biting jigs, I'm going to catch a quality bag of fish."

Fellow pro Mickey Bruce of Georgia says patience is a virtue of fishing jigs in nontraditional seasons.

"Most anglers don't give the jig enough time," he adds. "Although there are days when the jig can produce a lot of fish, its main attribute is that it produces BIG fish. But you've got to be patient, experiment with sizes, colors and techniques.

"I may go three hours without a bite, but I know that will change if I get the bait around a big bass."

The jig's effectiveness depends largely upon whether you've presented it properly and in the right area. Here's a look at some year-round tactics.

SPRING

As clearwater lakes progress from winter to spring, the jig is at its best, whether the fish are deep or shallow.

"Brushpiles, newly sprouted lily pads, rocks, pier posts and seawalls are my primary targets," explains Mark Zona, a Sturgis, Mich., pro who focuses on shallow water. "In the North, that pattern works extremely well when the water is below 50 degrees. Most people are fishing the dropoffs under that situation, but I find more aggressive bass in the shallows."

Zona says his best catches come in less than 3 feet of water, so he opts for a jig weighing 3/16 ounce or less. He tips it with either a pork frog or a plastic craw.

THE JIG will always be known for its prowess in cold water, but pros have proved it's a superb year-round lure, too.

ALTHOUGH JIGS are primarily used for shallow water applications, western pros have found them effective when bass are deep, as well.

"I don't believe in letting the bait sit still, either," he says. "Even though the fish aren't real aggressive, I've found that moving it steadily, with short hops, works better than a slow, methodical presentation."

The jig is equally effective during early spring on high water, stained lakes, adds Shuffield. He feeds jigs to staging bass around wood and brush in spawning coves on the northwest side of a lake. He prefers a slower fall, so he relies on jigs weighing less than 1/2 ounce and tips them with pork.

Veteran jig fisherman Basil Bacon of Springfield, Mo., says the prespawn season is one of the most overlooked by jig fishermen. Unlike traditionalists who opt for lighter jigs in cold water, he prefers to cast large jigs over chunk rock and gravel banks that form a shallow ledge along a dropoff.

"I throw a 5/8-ounce jig most of the time, because I think bass want a big bait," he explains. "The heavy jig works on the same principal as a Carolina rig, in that the more commotion you make and the more you stir up the bottom, the more it attracts the bass." Once bass begin to nest, jigs become less productive. But don't give up on them.

"I'll use finesse lures to aggravate the bass, then throw the jig in there to catch the fish," offers Shuffield. "When a bass grabs a jig, you stand a better chance of landing it than you do with other types of lures."

The postspawn period is tough for any type of lure, but the jig can be your best choice for fooling females. Even though the bigger bass seem nonexistent for a few days following the spawn, they're still around.

"They get tight to cover and won't chase a bait," says Shuffield. "I look for bass fry in the bushes and pitch my jig in the middle. The bass aren't aggressive, but if you put a jig in one's face, it will take it."

SUMMER

Shuffield believes summer is a prime time for jig fishing, yet few anglers realize that fact. Instead, most go with fast moving lures and worms on middepth structure. At the same time, Shuffield is casting jigs to channel ledges, humps and breaklines. If grass is available, he flips them through matted sections. In river arms, he flips jigs into shallow, thick cover.

Plastic vs. Pig

Do you use plastic trailers for your jig, or should you opt for pork? Here are the benefits for each, so choose according to your priorities:

PLASTIC
— Many colors available
— Many shapes and styles to choose from
— Inexpensive
— Not messy like pork

PORK
— Action is more lifelike
— Feels more like real baitfish
— Stays on hook longer
— Has long lasting scent and taste

"The jig is a good summer tool when the lake gets a lot of fishing pressure," he explains. "Find heavy cover in shallow water and put the jig in places other anglers ignore."

Bruce, meanwhile, likes to throw jigs to deep water targets during summer.

"Rattles and long hops are keys to making jigs work when you know bass are holding on deep structure," he explains. "Sometimes they hit while the jig is rising, but usually the strike comes on the fall."

Current also is a good place to fish summer jigs, says McIntosh. Largemouth and smallmouth will move into river current to feed around eddies of bridges, creek mouths and points. Current is packed with oxygen, and bass are accustomed to seeing crawfish wash into those areas.

FALL

There may be better lures for catching a quick limit when fish are aggressive, but the jig won't take a back seat to any bait when it comes to producing heavyweight bass. Jig experts keep one rigged even when they're working spinnerbaits and crankbaits in shad-packed creeks.

"The jig is your best choice for catching big bass around logs, stumps and other wood in the tributaries," explains Shuffield. "You also can work it rather quickly. This is one time of year when you can swim a jig off the bottom and catch quality bass."

The swimming technique works around other types of cover, too. Shuffield uses a 1/4-ounce jig tipped with a big No. 1 Uncle Josh pork frog and swims it beneath the surface around floating docks in creek or river arms.

"Twitch as you swim it along," he explains.

McIntosh says the swimming jig can be deadly in sparse lily pads in late fall. Once pads begin to die back, he swims a 3/8-ounce jig-and-pork on the surface. He allows the bait to fall into pockets or along the outside edge of the pads.

"It's a lot like fishing a Rat, except you can drop the bait beneath the surface," he explains. "Some-

REGARDLESS OF the season, a jig pitched into heavy cover is the best presentation for triggering strikes from big bass.

times you'll see the bass 'waking' toward the bait, and that's when you should let it fall — and hang on to your rod."

WINTER

Stanley Mitchell targets rivers for winter jigging. He looks for eddies close to the bank and pitches the jig into depths from 2 to 10 feet. He says river fish are the most active, yet they still prefer a slow moving bait.

"I use a 3/8-ounce jig if the current will allow it, and either a No. 11 or No. 1 Uncle Josh pork frog," the former Classic winner says. "The best spots are deep holes away from current, and if cover is there, it's even better. The fish will stack up on a spot like that throughout the winter."

Creek ledges and bluff banks also are good places to fish the jig in cold water. But don't overlook shallow cover during those multiday warming trends.

"If a fish is hungry, it's going to go shallow," insists McIntosh. "You'd be surprised how many bass can be caught on a jig in less than 3 feet of water that time of year."

Jig experts admit there are occasions when bass will ignore jigs. But because those occurrences are so rare, it's a bait worth trying under all conditions.

SWIMMING FOR TROPHY LARGEMOUTH

These oversize plastic baits have a unique swimming action that gives bass anglers the edge against huge bass . . .

SOUTHERN CALIFORNIA anglers locate likely structure — preferably close to where stocker trout have been released — and "camp out" in wait for big bass to show up. It can be tedious to throw a big swim bait repeatedly into the same spots, but the payoffs can be huge.

IN BASS FISHING TODAY, there are seemingly as many different lures as there are lakes and streams in which to fish them.

The mind-boggling rate at which new lures are introduced continues to accelerate. Bass enthusiasts are inventive folk, and nowhere is this more true than in Southern California, where a cult of big fish specialists is rewriting the definition of trophy size. And these anglers are constantly inventing new lures and techniques for getting at the biggest bass.

The latest entries in this "weapons race" for trophy bass are a group of large soft plastic lures called "swim baits," which are designed to mimic bigger baitfish. They follow the development of some highly successful hard-body and hybrid lures made for the same purpose. Few bass anglers anywhere are unaware of the Castaic Bait or the A.C. Plug, which imitate the rainbow trout planted in the same California waters that hold Florida-strain bass.

What is more, these baits will work throughout the country. Don't dismiss them merely as imitations of rainbow trout. These big baits can mimic any forage fish that grows to a large size, and they can trigger awesome strike responses from 10-pound bass anywhere you find them.

LOCATING LUNKERS

Because these lures are commonly used for bass that dine on winter-stocked trout, most anglers currently fish them mostly during the mild Southern California winters. Troy Folkestad, an experienced tournament angler and guide in Southern California, knows the rigors of fishing swim baits on heavily pressured lakes and thinks they are useful anytime.

"Swim baits definitely work better in winter,

but they will take bass year-round," Folkestad says. "Big bass are opportunistic feeders at any time of the year, and when they are in a chasing mood, they hunt large prey."

"The biggest bass stage off the points and chase schools of bait," notes Mike Gash. A tournament angler and expert swim bait angler, Gash plies his trade on many lakes but concentrates on swim bait fishing in winter on Lake Perris in Moreno Valley.

Last spring, Gash posted a number of trophy bass, including a pair weighing 13 pounds, 6 ounces and 12 pounds, 5 ounces on a single day of fishing with the Basstrix Swim Bait. He agrees with Folkestad that fishing swim baits only when trout are planted, and right at the point of stocking, is not necessary to get a trophy bass.

He also thinks that instead of hunting for big blips on the depthfinder, a better method of fishing swim baits might be to wait for the fish to find you.

"Big bass don't hold in any one area for very long," Gash points out. "They work the points and the beaches, hunting for schools of trout and anything else they can eat. If you hang out in a particular area that you know will have big bass at some time during the day, you'll see something happen. Sometimes as you come by an area, you'll see a concentration of big blips on the screen, but they aren't active, they're just hanging there."

Gash believes that whether or not you see big fish on a known spot, the trick with these large baits is to find a good spot and stick to it.

It's much like fishing live bait on structure. A bait fisherman might spend the entire day without a bite, but he knows from experience that, sooner or later, the larger bass will move in to feed. When that happens, if a bass sees a big meal swim by, the fish will nail it.

SWIM BAIT RETRIEVES

Gash knows that when big bass are right on the bottom, usually they are not very active — but if you get the bait in their strike zone, they'll eat it.

"If the fish are suspended, I throw the bait past them and rip it back through the area. As soon as the swim bait hits the water, I put the reel in gear and make my bait jump right out of the water. I can make it skip four or five times before it sinks. It looks like a frantic bait trying to get away. If you slap it down on the water, and just let it sink, it seems to throw the fish off."

This rapid retrieve gets rid of what he calls "sniffers" — bass that will follow a slower bait but won't bite. The ripping bait makes an aggressive fish hammer it. Sometimes it turns a sniffer into an eater.

"They aren't afraid of the boat either. If they want the bait, they'll eat it within 5 feet of me," he says. "They'll eat a swim bait when it's half out of the water."

Folkestad adds trolling to the mix, especially when he's guiding anglers who may not have fished the big baits before. How deep he works the swim bait depends both on the kind of structure and where the bass are holding. If the bass are right on the bottom, he makes sure the bait is bumping bottom as well. When trolling over a rocky point with big rocks and boulders, he wants the baits to swim higher, so they don't get hung up.

"It's really hard on your line to drag it over a big boulder pile," Folkestad notes. "You lose the feel of what the lure is doing, and it tears up the line." He often fishes swim baits on Berkley's FireLine instead of mono because the superline is much more sensitive.

"One trolling trick I use, most bass anglers don't know about," he reveals. "I jerk or twitch the rod almost constantly. It's a method used by trophy trout anglers who troll big Rapalas for monster brown trout."

He gives the rod a pump to move the bait forward a foot or two, then at the end of that movement, he twitches it sharply. This makes the bait behave erratically, jumping sideways and rolling on its side.

"It looks like the bait is in trouble, and that attracts a strike from a following bass," he explains.

SWIM BAITS come in a variety of sizes, but most are designed to resemble rainbow trout — the preferred food for giant bass in some Southern California reservoirs. Some brands have weighted hooks molded inside, while others are meant to be threaded onto a jighead.

TOPWATER

The twilight zone:
a place where bass rise
to surface lures,
or so we hope . . .

CHOOSING AND USING TOPWATER LURES
A guide to picking the right floating bait

B.A.S.S. PRO LARRY NIXON knows that topwaters rank high on the list of lure selection when a quality bass is needed.

K A-BOOSH!! Nothing tops the thrill of a big bass smashing a topwater lure! Here's how B.A.S.S. pros choose and use surface baits for lunkers, and limits of keepers as well.

WHEN & WHERE TO USE TOPWATER LURES

Postspawn through fall — Most bass experts begin casting surface baits in spring once the water temperature tops 65 degrees. This roughly coincides with the postspawn period, the time when bass leave their bedding areas and resume active feeding. The topwater bite normally continues through summer and fall, then diminishes once the water cools below 60 degrees in late autumn. But as with most bass fishing "rules," there are exceptions. On the Tournament Trail, big bass have been caught on stickbaits in 45 degree water, and on buzzbaits during snowstorms!

Around shallow cover — Bass hanging around shallow wood, weeds and rocks in reservoirs and natural lakes will often smash a lure, creating a ruckus on the surface, and can sometimes be provoked into striking by making repeated casts to a likely target.

On main lake structure — In clear lakes, bass often suspend around points, underwater humps and dropoffs and will swim surprising distances to strike a surface bait.

In streams and rivers — Bass in these environments are highly attuned to feeding on creatures swimming from one bank to another.

When bass are schooling — In summer and fall, large numbers of bass often chase baitfish to the surface, where a feeding frenzy takes place. Be alert for fish breaking water or birds circling and diving on injured baitfish. In this scenario, a topwater presentation is virtually guaranteed to draw a strike.

Topwater Styles

Surface baits come in many varieties, each designed for specific fishing situations. Make sure you have at least one of each style in your tacklebox.

■ **FLOATING MINNOW** — (Examples: Original Floating Rapala, A.C. Shiner, Bang-O-Lure) These subtle surface lures are most effective on bass in clear water, especially at the beginning and end of the topwater season. Pro's pointer: Try a floating minnow around bedding areas in shallow coves. Use a light action spinning outfit and 6- to 8-pound mono. Cast, twitch the rod tip gently, then let the lure rest several seconds before twitching it again.

■ **POPPER/CHUGGER** — (Hula Popper, Pop-R, Rattlin' Chug Bug) Distinguishing characteristics include a scooped-out face and a tail made of feathers or rubber strands. When the rod is jerked, the strands make a loud popping sound; some even spit water. Pro's pointer: Use poppers and chuggers when bass are holding in a confined area, such as in weedbeds growing just beneath the surface. Cast, pop the lure once or twice, then allow it to sit motionless.

■ **PROP BAIT** — (Devil's Horse, Tiny Torpedo, Woodchopper) Spinning propellers at one or both ends create maximum commotion when the lure is ripped repeatedly across the surface. Pro's pointer: Use a prop bait in choppy water and when it's overcast or raining. Retic frequently; the props can nick your line during casts.

■ **STICKBAIT/DARTING BAIT** — (Zara Spook, Sammy) An erratic lure requiring some skill on the angler's part to retrieve properly. Try it on large main lake structures such as points, humps and flats. Deadly on bass suspending in clear water. Pro's pointer: Fish a stickbait on a medium action 6-foot baitcasting rod with 14-pound mono. "Walk the dog" by snapping the line with sharp downward strokes of the rod tip while turning the reel handle with each stroke.

■ **WOBBLER** — (Jitterbug, Crazy Crawler) When reeled slowly and steadily, jerky side-to-side action creates maximum surface commotion to attract explosive strikes. Pro's pointer: Wobblers mimic live frogs. Retrieve 'em parallel to grassy banks in ponds and natural lakes, especially at daybreak and dusk.

■ **BUZZBAIT** — (Lunker Lure, Terminator Triple Buzz) Similar in construction to a spinnerbait, this is one of the noisiest surface lures. Use it in shallow water around laydown logs and grassy shorelines. Pro's pointer: Buzzbaits are big fish lures. Use stout tackle and heavy, abrasion-resistant line when fishing them.

■ **SCUM BAIT** — (Frogzilla, Rat) Usually made of soft plastic with upswept hooks, these critter mimics are designed to be crawled over lily pads and matted vegetation. Pro's pointer: Fish a frog or rat on a flipping stick with at least 20-pound mono. The long rod facilitates longer casts, lifts your line off the grass and helps power a lunker bass out of dense weeds and slop.

TARGETING POPPERS
Eliminate what works from what doesn't

WHEN ZELL ROWLAND won the B.A.S.S. Super Invitational on Tennessee's Lake Chickamauga in June 1986, popper, or chugger-style, baits were not on the radar screen. Even his winning lure, Rebel's P-60 Pop-R, had been relegated to the scrap heap several years before.

The small and close-mouthed cadre of professionals who were clued in to the chugger, a group that included such luminaries as Rick Clunn, were forced to scrounge their lures from tackle store bargain bins. A few with connections to the manufacturer and a willing crew of friends actually purchased 24-dozen lots — orders big enough for the factory to pull the molds out of mothballs.

Once the angling public got wind of what Rowland was up to, it became increasingly apparent that he had done far more than simply resurrect a forgotten lure: The lanky Texan had developed some rather far-reaching topwater strategy, using the chugger as its centerpiece.

At first, anglers focused on the spitting action made by Rowland's Pop-Rs — baits that were

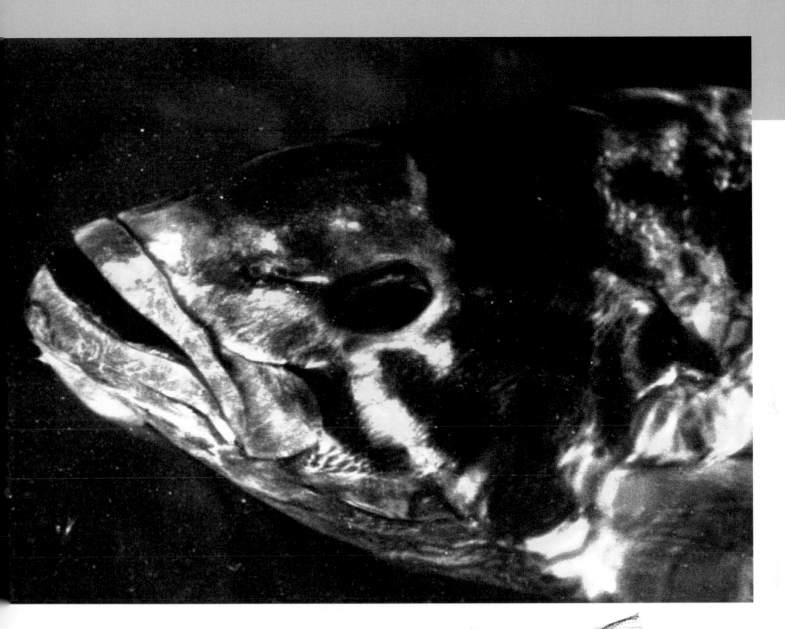

carefully sanded at the mouth to create less bite in the water as they were pulled along. While this shadlike spritz of water was extremely effective, Rowland has spent the intervening years trying to convince fishermen that it is but one part of the program.

"A lot of fishermen have molded into their brains that a bait must spit to catch a fish. This is not the key. It's the action you apply to the bait that matters. Sometimes a larger fish may want the bait fished extremely slow. If you work it slow, it's not going to spit, and will make a different sound," observes Rowland, who insists that the side-to-side dog walking retrieve is equally critical.

"It is a necessity, and it gives the bait more action. I teach people not to fall into the same

MOUTH DESIGN and body shape are the two primary factors to consider when choosing chuggers, and manufacturers have made sure there is a bait to suit every angler's preference.

More Flash From Poppers

Talk to Zell Rowland about chuggers, and you'll hear the word "flash" a hundred times more often than the word "color." Whether a lure is popped gently or chugged violently, the small flashes created mean more in drawing strikes than most any color scheme, no matter how lifelike the lure is.

"If I want more flash out of a bait, there are two things that I consider: the bottom color of the bait, and the mouth of the bait. This is what you're pulling; what goes under the water to create the disturbance.

"Often, if I want more flash, I'll paint the mouth solid white. Then, when I move the bait or chug it, the mouth digs into the water and throws a bigger flash than red or black."

routine. Before most anglers ever leave the house, they've tied their bait on the end of the rod. They've already determined the size of the line. When a professional angler practices, he will have about 14 rods

FISHING POPPERS around the edges of vegetation can be a very fruitful pattern during the summer months.

in his rod box, and every one will have a different pound-test. The lighter the line an angler uses, the more action he will get out of a chugger bait. Also, the bait will have more of a tendency to walk from left to right."

For instance, a move up from 10-pound test to 14 or 17 will produce a much tighter walking action. If this change in action doesn't affect the number of strikes, says Rowland, then stay with it.

"Rick Clunn taught me a lot in not only working topwater baits, but crankbaits as well. He always told me, 'If you get 10 strikes throwing 12-pound line, and you can get 10 strikes throwing 25-pound test, throw the 25!' " laughs Rowland.

Regardless of the line test, using the right rod is of utmost importance. For Rowland, this means an extremely limber rod — one that leans more to the parabolic side of the spectrum.

"It takes the 'dummy' away from the angler. It keeps you from being too fast, because it's more similar to a cranking rod that David Fritts might use. It allows a fish another second to pull the bait under before you ever set the hook.

"Remember, it's not how hard you set the hook; it's a matter of sharp hooks. Once the rod loads up, it applies enough pressure to cause a hook set."

However, none of this popping, chugging or dog walking makes any difference if a fisherman isn't in the right area doing the right thing.

"We always try to develop one pattern and let that be the strong suit of the tournament we're fishing. To me, being able to pattern a 4- or 5-pound fish is a lot easier

than trying to pattern a 2-pounder. I know where those better quality fish are laying on a stretch of grass, point or down a weedline.

"More than likely, when I catch a 3- or 4-pounder, it was sitting on a certain piece of cover next to a certain water depth. Or it was sitting on the edge of a grassline with some irregularity. I'll make note of where that fish came from. Then I'll run down another stretch of bank and be looking for that same scenario."

Rowland's confidence in his patterning methods is based on the belief that smaller fish feed more often and roam around more willingly than do larger bass.

"I think a bigger fish is more territorial than a 2-pounder. A 2-pounder may roam around, up and down a two-mile stretch of bank. I think a fish that weighs between 3 and 10 pounds doesn't roam that much. I think it sticks around one certain, little area."

Having identified the specifics of a pattern, Rowland then applies that information to his casting presentations. At the heart of his methodology is carefully making casts to areas he has designated as "sweet spots" — high percentage zones near targets that hold the greatest likelihood for success.

Although he avoids fan casting, he doesn't restrict himself to any one retrieve speed or cadence. This is still a work in progress until enough fish have convinced him of the most productive retrieve.

"The biggest mistake most anglers make when throwing any kind of chugger is watching me, Rick Clunn or Kevin VanDam on television and paying more attention to the fish we catch than to how we are working the bait."

Rowland's insistence on mastering the big picture items of location and presentation should not be taken as encouragement to neglect the details. In the world of chuggers, the little things do mean a lot.

Of these, one absolute in rigging, notes Rowland, is the addition of a feathered trailer. To him, it is integral to the action and flash, something that should be a part of every chugger presentation.

Choosing between the various chugger sizes is another area of concern — one that Rowland says is largely dependent on the size of the baitfish present. While this is often the best guideline, there are times when bass simply prefer one size to the next. To solve that dilemma, Rowland lets the bass be the final arbitrators.

"I let the fish tell me."

This Texas-bred professional is equally direct when addressing the argument over color, a concern that often adds more questions than necessary to the issue. His answer is both simple and straightforward.

"There are only three shades that fish can see, whether it's an ocean, river, pond or lake. These are dark, light and red. There isn't a fish that swims that doesn't have a darker back and a lighter bottom — and they all have red gills.

"When I'm throwing a topwater, the bottom is light in color whether it's bone, white or chrome. It's the easiest color for the fish to see. In off-colored water, the flash of silver has a tendency to disappear vs. something darker, such as chartreuse or black. These colors seem to create a better silhouette than chrome."

In all of this, the balance comes in sweating the details without letting them overwhelm you. For Rowland, it is a matter of experience and then paying attention to that experience. The goal? To eliminate what works from what doesn't.

MANY PROS feel that poppers are more effective when the rear treble is dressed with feather vs. plastic. The feather comes alive in the water, giving the rigid bait a lifelike appearance while sitting still.

WHILE THE FIRST prop baits were made of wood, most are now made of plastic. Both types are effective bass getters.

(Opposite page) ALTHOUGH MANY topwater baits work best on supercalm days, prop baits really shine when there is a slight chop on the water.

DON'T OVERLOOK PROP BAITS

How to put a new spin on topwater fishing

FOR WHATEVER REASON, surface lures adorned with propellers never have garnered the widespread acclaim lavished on poppers. Prop baits enjoy regional prominence, at best, even though a handful of career anglers dote on these lures.

"The prop bait gets a fair amount of attention in some areas," says noted bass pro Jim Bitter, "such as my home state of Florida. But it's generally overlooked, even among the pros. It just happens to be the one topwater bait that I use most."

Bitter's favorite prop bait, a 1/2-ounce Devil's Horse, exhibits the most basic prop bait design, which is a wooden cigar-shape body sporting a small, free-spinning metal propeller fore and aft. It casts well and the blades churn an arousing "bri-i-i-ip/bri-i-i-ip" ditty when the lure jukes across the surface.

The sound generated by the propellers is what distinguishes a prop bait from other topwater offerings. Large props kick up more ruckus than smaller ones, but they all serve to get a bass' attention. A subtle retrieve mimics the sound of a baitfish slapping the surface. A more lively action makes the blades erupt with a noise similar to that of a surface-feeding fish.

While the first prop baits were made of wood, many excellent versions are constructed of plastic. They range in shape from long and slender to short and fat, and they generally come in sizes 3/8, 1/2, 5/8 and 3/4 ounce.

In addition to Smithwick's Devil's Horse, some popular models include Cordell's Crazy Shad and Boy Howdy, Heddon's Dying Flutter, the Jumper from Gilmore Sales Co., Luhr Jensen's Nip-I-Diddee, Ozark Mountain's Woodchopper, Poe's Ace-In-The-Hole and Strike King's Prop Scout.

In contrast to the standard prop bait, tail-spin baits have no front propeller. This generally reduces the noise, but some tail-spin models kick up a fuss that is equal to double-spin prop baits. The tail-spin design gives a lure more freedom to dart from side to side and eliminates a common problem with standard prop baits — line tangling in the front propeller.

Popular single-spin prop baits include the Arbogast Snooker, Bagley's Injured Minnow, Luhr Jensen's Dalton

Finesse Props

When bass prefer a subtle topwater presentation, Kentucky pro Mike Auten turns to prop baits with a single spinner on the tail. These baits don't create the disturbance of double-prop versions, and can be made to go side-to-side with small twitches of the rod tip. Auten lets the bait sit for several seconds between twitches to create his finesse retrieve.

Pitching Prop Baits

When you see Tommy Biffle pitching to shoreline cover from a distance, it's natural to assume that the lure on the end of his line is a jig or soft plastic bait, such as a lizard or craw. Look closer and you may be shocked to find that Biffle is pitching a topwater lure.

"I throw a Gilmore Jumper on a 7-foot pitching stick with 20-pound Stren," says Biffle. "The long rod casts that heavy plug a good ways, and when I come to a dock or overhanging limb, I can pitch it under the cover."

When pitching a prop bait, Biffle does not grasp the plug at any time, as some anglers do with jigs and soft plastic baits. After retrieving the prop bait, he leaves an appropriate length of line for pitching and simply swings the lure back and pitches it forward in one smooth motion.

Nothing to it, if you're Tommy Biffle. Most everyone else will need practice.

Special, Heddon's Tiny Torpedo, Ozark Mountain's Ripper and the Sam Griffin Jerk-N-Sam.

Bagley's Spinner Tail Bang-O-Lure and Bandit's Stick Bait combine a floating minnow body and a tail prop. These lures work especially well in the spring when bass are shallow, and whenever bass prefer a quieter presentation.

HITTING THE HOLES

Bitter ties on a Devil's Horse anytime bass are susceptible to a topwater lure, especially when he fishes in Florida. He uses it most often, however, in the spring.

"It's great during spawning time," he says, "mainly because you're fishing clear, shallow water."

When fishing Florida in the spring, Bitter seeks shallow, protected spawning areas. If the vegetation isn't too dense, Bitter starts out with a jerkbait, his favorite lure and the one he is noted for fishing. He opts for a prop bait when the vegetation is too thick for a jerkbait.

"In heavy vegetation," says Bitter, "you'll find beds in little open pockets. I just pitch a Devil's Horse into a hole, zip it a couple of times and let it rest. A lot of times, the longer you let it sit, the bigger the fish and the more bites you get. If I don't get a bite, I jerk it out and hit another hole."

The small targets place a premium on casting accuracy. Bitter eschews the long, double-grip rods preferred by many other pros in favor of a 5 1/2-foot medium heavy baitcasting rod that features a pistol grip. The little rod lends itself to the underhand roll cast, which is just the thing for slinging a prop bait precisely to the back of a pothole.

Wrestling big bass out of thick weeds with a short rod and a treble-hook lure may appear to be an overwhelming task, but Bitter takes it in stride. Since he uses 20-pound monofilament when fishing prop baits, he isn't concerned about breaking off.

"I just hang on," he says. "A lot of times they snub up against the vegetation and you have to go get them."

Kentucky pro Mike Auten also enjoys his most consistent success with a prop bait when bass frequent spawning areas. He believes most of the bass that strike it at this time are postspawners that are either guarding fry or cruising the shallows in search of a meal.

"I've made a lot of big catches with the Bang-O-Lure (with rear prop) on Kentucky Lake in May and the first part of June, right after the bass come off the beds," says Auten. "I work it around bushes in the backs of coves and on spawning flats where most other guys flip jigs and cast spinnerbaits.

"I think of it as a finesse prop bait," he continues. "I barely twitch it, and let it rest two or three seconds at a time. Sometimes you have to let it sit longer. I'm not really

The Buzz About Prop Baits

Anglers having a problem getting a good hook set with a buzzbait should turn to a prop bait with two spinners. The amount of surface commotion caused by the double prop is similar to a buzzbait; you can stop a prop bait in the strike zone so bass have a better chance to strike it solidly; and the treble hooks are more likely to snag a bass than the single, upturned hook of a buzzbait.

BIG PROP BAITS, such as this Gilmore Jumper, catch big bass for anglers who know how and where to use them.

a patient fisherman, but that can be deadly."

Auten's slowdown tactics also have produced good catches for him in spring B.A.S.S. tournaments by working the Bang-O-Lure over sandy spots in hydrilla beds on Lake Seminole, and by pulling bass from submerged stumps on Alabama's Neely Henry Lake.

When Auten believes he is dealing with especially temperamental bass, he drops down to a 4 1/4-inch Spinner Tail Bang-O-Lure, which he fishes on spinning tackle and 12-pound-test line. Regardless of the lure size, Auten's primary colors include chartreuse, gold/black back and Tennessee shad.

BIG BASS BAITS

Mark Menendez, another Kentucky pro, also enjoys success with a Spinner Tail Bang-O-Lure. But he generally catches bigger bass on a wooden 5/8-ounce Gilmore Jumper or a plastic 3/8-ounce Boy Howdy. The Jumper carries better and gets the nod when Menendez must cast into the wind.

"I really don't throw them but about two times of the year: during postspawn and again in fall," Menendez says. "I probably use them more in the fall than any other time."

In the fall, Menendez fishes prop baits over stump flats, stakebeds and other visible cover in the backs of coves where bass have followed shad into the shallows. These fish are hit hard with spinnerbaits and buzzbaits, but they rarely see a prop bait.

"It's such a different presentation from what everybody else is doing," says Menendez. "That's why bass get so aggressive toward a prop bait."

On clear lakes that produce good smallmouth, Menendez drops down to a 3/8-ounce Jumper, which he believes draws more strikes and is easier for the bass to engulf. In September and October, he targets pea gravel points and steep rocky banks on the main lake. His boat may at times be sitting in 25 feet of water, but most of the bass come up from water no deeper than 12 feet.

"In clear water, the farther you throw the bait, the better off you are," says Menendez. To help in setting the hook at long distances, he uses 20-

pound monofilament and a 6 1/2-foot rod, "which has a little bit of tip in it and a lot of backbone."

Prime prop bait conditions for Menendez include overcast days and whenever a breeze puts a 6- to 10-inch chop on the surface, both conducive to fishing main lake areas that are well away from the bank.

"In clear water, bass tend to follow the bait," says Menendez. "I've had them try to take it away from me right at the boat. Just when you think you're through and you start cranking the lure back, that's when they'll often nail it. That burst of speed sometimes turns them on.

"You'll often see bass slapping at these baits," he adds. "And a lot of times fish come up and just nip the back end. If the hooks are real sharp, you can catch these fish."

If prop baits are so deadly, why don't they attract more advocates? Probably because they require slower presentations and more patience than do other lures. Menendez and other pros who dote on prop baits don't mind that these lures haven't received the celebrity they deserve. They would just as soon keep a good thing to themselves.

Tuning Props

Controlling the forward movement of a prop bait is a crucial element of every cast. While this motion is largely dependent on rod and reel work, the props themselves can deliver a welcome assist.

For longer, more exaggerated bait movements, bend the props back slightly. (This reduces the resistance of water on the bait.)

By doing the opposite and bending the prop blades forward, the bait is restricted and moves only slightly forward.

SURFACE DARTERS: UNSUNG TOPWATERS

These sashaying, dog-walking surface baits are catching bass from coast to coast, or hadn't you heard?

E VEN BEFORE THE RIPPLES SUBSIDE on a topwater strike at Lake Fork or Table Rock or Mead, the word has already leaked out. Right down to the specifics of how to fish the lure and where to get it, bass fishermen rarely let something new slip through their informal, yet remarkably efficient, bass fishing intranet. But it does happen.

In fact, it seems to have happened to a certain topwater category that has a number of accomplished and loyal practitioners, but a profile lower than the Mid-Atlantic Trench. Normally, such anonymity is well-deserved in a sport where hype will sell a bait once, but the lack of performance keeps it on the shelf forever.

However, in the case of surface-darting baits, there seems to be more at work than the standard economic forces of supply and demand.

The baits — which can "walk the dog" more enticingly than the much revered Zara Spook — slipped in from Japan in decidedly minuscule quantities. Shortly after the balsa Sammy disappeared, a plastic version debuted in three

THE BANANALIKE bend of many darting baits makes walking-the-dog action easier for anglers to produce.

sizes, sporting premium hooks and internal rattles. And, just as Folkestad swears allegiance to the original, Greg Hines, another B.A.S.S. pro from the West (and someone who forged his early reputation on his prowess with the Zara Spook), places great faith in these plastic versions.

In the West, the trend toward the more finesse-style surface darters, observes Hines, was actually instigated by the larger, heavier lures used in the East. With clear water and sometimes heavy fishing pressure, western fishermen knew they needed

something with the same dog-walking action, but in a lighter, more subtle version. Something that could withstand clear water scrutiny, didn't set down with a heavy splash and could be worked very slowly.

For all those reasons — and the fact that the bait pushes water rather than skittering over it — Hines finds the plastic models very effective. Not to mention that the three sizes allow him to "match the hatch" without sacrificing the action.

The Sammy hasn't cornered the surface-darter market, by any means. Bagley has the Rattlin' Twitcher, a 4-inch darter made of balsa that approximates the Sammy's shape and walking action. In addition, a slew of new walking/darting baits has poured in from the Far East, including Yo-Zuri's superpremium Walk'n Dog stickbait.

One BASSMASTER touring pro who is quite content to use something other than a Sammy is John Murray, an Arizona pro who has used the Rico Suavé for nearly five years. Designed by Norio Tanabe, the Rico Suavé (called the Splash

MOST DARTING BAITS, like this Lucky Craft Sammy, contain rattles within the body of the lure to help attract bass from longer distances.

How To Walk The Dog

The proper way to fish a darting bait is in a zigzag pattern: After it touches down, hold the rod down and to the side, then begin rhythmically twitching the rod tip to the side while intermittently turning the reel handle a half-turn at a time. The key is allowing some slack in the line, which permits the bait to glide in one direction. Twitching again makes it glide in the opposite direction.

At the beginning of a long cast, it may be necessary to begin retrieving with the rod tip raised slightly; gradually lower the tip as the bait approaches the boat until the rod is pointed almost directly downward.

Timing is everything. It takes practice and a little coordination for an angler to establish the right cadence of rod twitches and reel turns. While learning the technique, begin with slow, deliberate movements of the rod and reel handle. Gradually speed up both actions until the bait is walking and spitting uniformly.

Walking baits work best on medium action rods with fast tips and with 12- to 14-pound-test line.

To work the bait with a minimum of forward progress, move the rod tip with shorter twitches and without reeling. When too much slack develops in the line, reel in a few feet and repeat.

Sometimes the best action is no action. If walking a lure by bassy-looking cover or over suspended fish a few times fails to produce, suddenly stop the lure and let it rest for 30 seconds or longer. You'll be amazed at how many times bass (particularly smallmouth) will rise to blast a stationary lure.

THE SLENDER PROFILE of this Yo-Zuri Walk'n Dog makes it zigzag in a tighter pattern than larger baits.

Pencil in Japan) basically evolved from the Japanese design criteria of producing a more subtle version of an already popular lure style.

"There are a lot of baits now coming out of Japan in that Sammy genre. They have an action like a Slug-Go in that they don't do the same thing twice," observes Murray.

"I've always used the Suavé and other baits which have a nice action like a Spook. The Sammy and some others started into the other phase of random action. Personally, I don't want a lot of random action because I tend to miss fish on them. I like to get some sort of cadence going with whatever topwater or subsurface lure I'm throwing."

While there may be a lack of consensus among the top western pros about which bait to fish, the applications for these surface darters are fairly clear-cut. In terms of water clarity, the clearer the better since this is the one factor that pushes the effectiveness of these lures beyond other surface lures. However, as Murray counsels, the shallower the water, the more off-colored it can be and still generate excellent results.

In postspawn conditions where the fish are not ready to chase and don't want a lot of noise associated with the lure, the surface darters now do the work in western waters where minnow baits like the Rapala once were king. During the postspawn period, the retrieve is slow and methodical around the outside parts of coves, over deeper brush, around cliffs adjacent to spawning flats or where shallow areas afford deep water access. At times, a large, sweeping, side-to-side sashay is what draws strikes. In other situations, a tight, restricted, back-and-forth motion makes the difference. Perhaps the best strategy is to begin with the standard walk-the-dog medium retrieve and then let the fish reveal how they want it worked.

As the season moves into summer, pressured fishing conditions also create opportunities for surface darters that create noise by the movement of the lure itself, as opposed to a cupped face or buzz blade.

"This subtle action, especially in heavy-pressured water, makes a difference," notes Murray. "In recent years at Lake Mead, for instance, these baits

WHETHER USING large cigar-shaped baits, or some of the smaller minnow-shaped darting baits, an angler's objective should be the same: Imitate a wounded baitfish.

have been very strong — particularly during the latter days of events when most fishermen have been pounding the water with Ricos, buzzbaits and such."

The "pressure" factor also comes into play in dealing with large schools of shad and the competition from this natural food source. The smaller, natural appearance of the surface darters more closely duplicates the forage and — when combined with a somewhat quicker, more frantic retrieve — brings together both feeding and reactive responses.

In the late summer and early fall, the retrieve is speeded up to produce a textbook reaction bite where quick movements can elicit strikes from bass moving back into coves and around brush.

Of course, when you have a bait with the speed range and individuality of a surface darter, the rules about how fast or slow to work it (or how erratically) are certainly not set in concrete. And, as John Murray points out, this can be as much an advantage as a disadvantage.

"It's a harder lure to fish; there is no single right way to work it. With a Rico (popper), you simply throw it out, twitch it twice and a fish will come get it. With this lure, you really can't do it that way. You have to find the cadence and retrieve that works for the day. And, this will change with the conditions, either day-to-day or even hour-to-hour. So, you have to do some experimenting."

When it comes to picking the ideal conditions for surface darters, Murray prefers a calm and glassy surface for his Suavé. To him, this is precisely the reason for their design. If the wind picks up, he will generally switch to a bait that draws more attention.

For Hines, the prime situation is clear water with fish holding in the 10- to 15-foot range, or whenever he's working over vast expanses of scattered vegetation and can't possibly make a cast to every little hole or notch in the grass. In these conditions, Hines can make his Sammy do double duty by alternately working it across the larger

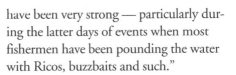
SURFACE DARTERS work great in the West, and other places where fishing pressure is heavy.

areas to attract fish and slowing down to twitch it over small pockets.

One important key to fishing surface darters that generally measure 4 inches or less is the correct rod action. With these baits, the optimum rod is one with enough length and power to cast the lure effectively, but a limber enough tip to work the bait without pulling it.

Both Hines and Murray opt for rods in the 7-foot class, with Hines using a 7 1/2-foot medium to medium-light Quantum Tour Edition and Murray employing a 7-foot, light action Shimano rod. While Hines may go to Berkley Fire-Line to reduce the line diameter, Murray pretty much sticks to 15-pound Berkley Big Game.

In all of this, perhaps the most perplexing question is "Why haven't the surface darter lures become more popular?" Apparently, they solve some of the drawbacks to other topwater lures in subtlety and action. They've proved themselves in the toughest "test tanks" of the West. And some of the big name pros in the East have fallen under their spell. So, what's up?

For most anglers, John Murray's assessment is probably quite accurate: Like a ballplayer who waits on the bench behind big name stars, the only reason no one has heard from his bat or glove is the absence of his name on the daily lineup card.

SOFT PLASTIC JERKBAITS: FROM TOP TO BOTTOM

Sometimes, bass prefer a delicate presentation

DESPITE MANY ADVERTISING CLAIMS to the contrary, a truly innovative lure is a rare commodity. Most are simply subtle alterations of existing baits and have relatively little effect on how fishermen catch bass.

Among the noteworthy exceptions to this rule is Lunker City's Slug-Go, the soft jerkbait that rocketed onto the angling scene in the early 1990s.

Like a minimalist, modern piece of art, the Slug-Go's simplicity went against the grain of lure-making excess. Perhaps fortunate for Herb Reed and his invention, the deceptively unremarkable design of this bait did not hamper its marketing, since many anglers had already heard of its near instant, on-the-water success before ever really seeing one.

In short order, the Slug-Go generated a tidal wave of clones from other manufacturers. At the same time, a legion of anglers discovered a whole new lure category. From this powerful kick-start, bass fishermen set about pioneering and refining their techniques for fishing what has become standard issue in every bass angler's arsenal.

SOFT JERKBAITS match the profile and texture of baitfish. The real key to their success, though, is the erratic way they move when twitched.

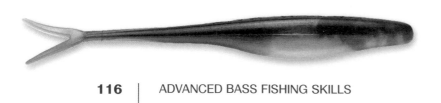

DELICATE, BUT DEADLY

To truly appreciate the potential of a soft jerkbait, a fisherman first needs to understand its strengths.

Without question, the primary application for plastic jerkbaits is in clear to slightly stained water from the surface down to six feet. With a 4/0 or 5/0 offset, wide gap hook rigged Texas style, these plastics are extremely effective in situations where hard plastic versions are ignored by wary bass or the presence of cover precludes the use of anything with treble hooks.

For California pro Randy Best, the beauty of soft jerkbaits comes in the delicacy of presentation.

"Although I've used them year-round, they are very productive in prespawn conditions when fish

are real shallow," he says. "Even when fish are at their spookiest, you can cast a bait onto the bank and slide it into the water without any disturbance. Since it doesn't drop to the bottom very quickly, the bait seems to hang in the area for a while, just tempting fish to respond."

Having nothing more than a minnow-shaped hunk of plastic to work with, however, an angler must rely on his skill to impart the right action.

"With these lures, every day is a new learning experience in gauging the aggressiveness of the fish and finding the right presentation for the conditions," observes Terry Baksay, a Connecticut B.A.S.S. tournament veteran who helped bring the Slug-Go to national prominence.

In many situations, he has found soft jerkbaits work best when they are twitched beneath the surface.

"In general, I think most people fish them too fast, especially near the surface," he says. "To me, a bass is really going out on a limb when it pursues a bait on the surface. When going after one

WHETHER YOU'RE fishing small waters or big lakes, shallow water bass are bound to go for soft jerkbaits. Postspawn is prime time for these lures.

that's 2 or 3 feet down, they don't feel quite as threatened."

Of equal importance is mixing up retrieve speeds to find the most productive pace, counsels Mike O'Shea, a Western tournament pro and guide.

Speed, though, is only one part of the equation. Finding the right cadence also is important, and that's not always so easy, since anglers don't "feel" a soft jerkbait as much as they "sense" it.

"When you pull the rod, there is no real weight at the other end," Best says. "A soft twitch will make the bait jump a considerable distance. Without much feedback or lure contact, this bait requires some dedication and experience to really learn how to fish it."

BALANCE IMPORTANT

Along those lines, balanced tackle and careful rigging play an important role in realizing the potential of these remarkable lures. Chief among these considerations is a medium/heavy to heavy action rod that provides enough power for solid hook sets and adequate tip action to feel connected to a relatively light bait.

Evolution Of Jerkbaits

The original soft jerk-baits were little more than blunt, straight worms. Lures like these, which are made to resemble shad and other baitfish, have become increasingly popular. They are meant to be fished on a 3/0 or 4/0 wide gap hook and without a weight. Even without a sinker, they're heavy enough to be thrown on baitcasting tackle.

Although many anglers employ braided lines in heavy cover, most will opt for monofilament whenever they can get away with it. This preference stems from the fact that the nonstretching superlines can cause an angler to move the bait too far or with too much force, which makes it much tougher to pause on the hook set. This momentary hesitation is critical to allow the bass time to turn away and therefore ensure a positive set.

In most cases, line tests range from 15 to 20 pounds. In ultraclear water, though, O'Shea feels that monofilament as light as 10-pound gives him the right blend of performance and power.

"The Owner hooks I use are so darn sharp, I really haven't experienced many problems in hook setting," he says. "Plus, if you're fishing in open water, you can always leave the hook point exposed to tip the scales in your favor."

WEIGHTING THE BAIT

While adding weight to soft jerkbaits has always been part of the program, fishermen continually are trying new methods for doing so. For most anglers, weight is added using lead nails or solder inserted vertically through the body and trimmed flush with the plastic. The amount and position of these weights can be altered to affect the sink rate and the

Floating Worms Are Super For Summer

In the heat of summer, most fishermen plan to be on the water at sunup and again at sundown, with a siesta in between. After trying this sizzling summer trick, however, you might become a midday bass angler.

It works throughout summer on lakes with canopy cover, such as docks and breakwalls made of floating tires. Rig a floating worm with a 2/0 or 3/0 worm hook, and tie it to a spinning rig. Soft jerkbaits and conventional plastic worms will work, too, but they sink differently than a floating worm, and they're not as productive.

Cast to the edge of the floating tires or dock and let the lure sink. If fish are holding near the surface, they'll ambush the lure right away. If they're holding a bit deeper, in the 4- to 5-foot range, you can make the worm sink a little faster by inserting a piece of finishing nail in the plastic.

The technique works best in slightly off-color water, especially on lakes that do not stratify in summer, or ones with a very shallow thermocline. While the action takes place at or near the surface, canopy cover suspended over deep water is best. Bright days and a slight breeze complete the pattern.

attitude of the descent (horizontal or nose-down).

When weather changes, heavy fishing pressure or other factors make bass inactive, Baksay recommends putting weight in the middle of the lure to create a slow, horizontal fall. For more active bass or when working deeper, a weight-forward lure stays down easier and can be worked faster, if desired.

In addition to adding weights for better performance, the main modifications in soft jerkbait strategies now have to do with working the lures deeper than normal.

If nothing else, simply getting below that narrow subsurface range opens up a lot of untapped water and broadens the seasonal applications for these lures.

"More and more people are starting to fish them deeper because they're realizing that fish have not been exposed to these lures down in 10 to 15 feet of water," counsels Baksay.

That is not to say that deeper fish are necessarily more active, so it's necessary to keep a soft jerkbait securely within a fairly confined strike zone.

A nose-weighted lure, which does not tend to rise on the retrieve, often fills the bill. It enables a fisherman to keep the lure deeper through much of the presentation. The problem with fishing an internally weighted jerkbait is that it can take so long for the lure to descend to the proper depth. A coverage technique it is not.

Even less of a search method — but one that can pay off handsomely when fish are precisely located — is a soft jerkbait tactic known as "deadsticking." In this technique, the bait is allowed to sink near an outside weedline or rocky structure and lie there for as long as the angler can bear to wait.

Deadsticking relies on the ability of these lures to produce strikes under the toughest of circumstances. With only a minimum of movement, the soft jerkbait most likely duplicates the subtle struggling of a dying or injured baitfish.

FOLLOW-UP APPLICATIONS

Of the nontraditional methods for soft jerkbaits, the most effective and proven technique has been in topwater follow-up presentations. Although many baits have been touted in this role, the soft jerkbait could easily be placed atop the list. It works great as a comeback lure for the very reasons it's so productive in other situations: a subtle entry, a slow fall and the capability of delivering action without being moved too quickly out of the strike zone.

"I feel that a soft jerkbait is the finest follow up lure for topwater situations that you can possibly use," notes Baksay. "The fish has just reacted to something, and before that mood changes, here comes something that looks like what they originally expected to grab."

Among the newer applications for soft jerkbaits are those involving flipping and Carolina rigging.

Flipping incorporates elements of deadsticking, since the bait skates slowly to the bottom and then is subtly twitched out of the cover. In many cases, the strikes come when the bait gently darts and ricochets as it emerges from the cover.

The technique that may offer more far-reaching opportunities, however, is Carolina rigging. With the bait separated from the weight, the soft jerkbait can move about freely and offer a real departure from the normal Carolina rig/plastic lizard combination.

ADD A STINGER HOOK to a surface frog, and you'll increase your hookups. Insert a 4/0 wide gap hook through the back of the frog so the point rides up, then tie the hook eye to the eye of the factory hooks.

FISH A FAKE FROG FOR SUMMER BASS
Skimming the surface for weedbed bass

I T'S 100-PLUS DEGREES, the sun is directly overhead and you're soaked with sweat. The prop of your trolling motor pulls effortlessly through glassy waters unmarked by even the hint of a breeze. An ocean of Gatorade couldn't quench your thirst. For some, this is the perfect definition of bass fishing hell.

To others, like Joe Thomas, Jim Munk and Bobby Barrack, it's very much the opposite.

For these aficionados of the Snag Proof frog, hot weather, a high sun and calm waters are precisely the elements required for superb topwater action. In the world of these bassin' "frogmen," the term "doldrums" means only one thing: While other anglers sip lemonade at the marina, they alone will be hammering bass.

Contrary to popular opinion, the so-called "summer doldrums" do not erase fishing opportunities, but only increase them anywhere floating mats of vegetation or shade pockets along tule lines exist.

For eastern anglers like B.A.S.S. touring pro Joe Thomas, these opportunities are nearly as abundant as the lakes themselves. For western pros like Jim Munk and Bobby Barrack, one only need look to northern California's Clear Lake or the Delta for these midsummer daydreams.

"People may not believe it, but some of the best times during the summer — from July to September — are anywhere from 10:30 a.m. to 3 p.m.," notes Munk, a tournament pro and guide.

"The high sun actually isolates the fish and places them in very predictable locations — in shaded areas and underneath the mats. Instead of cruising the shoreline and chasing bait, the bass will be sitting in the shadows, waiting for it to come to them."

Although floating mats of moss or milfoil may be intimidating to some anglers, they actually provide an ideal midsummer environment for both prey and predator alike. To Barrack, someone who knows the thousand miles of Delta tidal waterway better than

(Opposite page) THICK, IMPENETRABLE vegetation is no barrier to a die-hard bass angler like California's Bobby Barrack, who pulls bass out of the weeds with a floating frog.

Frog Colors

Color makes a difference, frogmen say. Use white or chartreuse frogs on cloudy days, and black or dark green on bright, sunny days, says pro angler Joe Thomas. Other fishermen doctor their frogs by painting dots of contrasting colors on the bellies of their frogs.

most know their own backyards, moss mats are very much like the solar blankets used on swimming pools. While the upper inch or two of water directly beneath the mat may be very warm, the water temperature can drop dramatically a foot or so below the surface.

In addition to providing a comfortable thermal environment, the mats also offer a unique blend of light penetration and camouflaging darkness from which largemouth can launch surprise attacks. Through visual clues, surface disturbance and vibration, bass sitting under these dense mats are precisely aware of what is taking place on the surface.

"It's like a mugger in a dark alley. Bass are able to lie under a dark mat and be completely camouflaged, yet also be able to look up or out into the light, like they're watching a television screen," observes Thomas.

"They know the bait is coming. They can hear it, and they can feel it."

DECISIONS, DECISIONS

Perhaps the toughest thing in fishing frogs is simply deciding which mats and which parts of these floating blankets will produce fish most consistently.

Since even moderate breezes can play havoc with the best-laid plans, Barrack first looks for areas that can be fished effectively even if the wind is blowing 20 miles per hour. Areas protected from the wind or positioned on the same side as the prevailing breeze are best.

"If you try to go against the grain in places where the wind has been hammering a bank for two or three days," warns Barrack, "you'll be facing moss that is 4 to 6 inches thick. Since the blanket is still intact, the fish won't move. But it's tough to fish that stuff. You'll get some of the greatest rolls of your life, but you won't catch them."

Once you've put yourself in the general area, the next step is finding the key fish-holding areas under a mat or along a reed line. Some of this diagnosis should be conducted in May or June, before the moss sets up. That way, an angler can locate the deeper areas within a grassbed. Generally, sparse weed growth will be the key to locating these zones.

"It's like fishing creek channels on a lake. You want the point that extends closest to the channel," counsels Barrack. "It's the same thing with moss. You want the moss closest to the deepest water available. In addition to the deep water, you will have some exposed sand where the weeds don't grow and holes are created where the bass can thrive."

Thomas, meanwhile, keys on less obvious irregularities, casting parallel to the weed edge to pluck off the most aggressive bass. Then, he works his way deeper over the mat by making casts at 45 degree angles, like he's cutting apart half a pie.

"Most of the time, I'm throwing to the thickest stuff I can find," he explains. "But if I can find a hole or two, these seem to be very productive strike zones."

PRESENTATIONS VARY

While the basics of where to find bass under mats and around cover are fairly consistent, the presentations required to draw strikes can vary greatly.

Pros' Choice

Snag Proof's Tournament Frog features rubber strands that act as swimming legs when the frog is moved. The high-floating bait and similar hollow body lures ride over vegetation, including algae and duckweed, drawing strikes from bass lurking in the shade beneath the weeds.

Munk prefers casting to open water beyond the mat, in hopes of drawing a strike, before pulling the frog up onto the vegetation. Once the lure is on the mat, he might pause for a count of five or 10. He repeats this procedure on the front edge of the mat so a bass has plenty of time to target the bait — and strike — when it comes off the edge.

Munk regularly fishes northern California's Clear Lake, which offers a blend of tules and grass clumps, but not the textbook mats of other areas. He has adjusted his technique to fit the situation. In this case, he looks for a small tule point with a grass clump in front that juts out into the main lake, sweeps back toward shore and juts out again, forming a small, tule-lined cove.

"First, fish the weed clump," he advises. "Then go right to the tules by casting to open water past the point, bringing the frog right to the point and letting it sit. Sometimes you can actually see the tules being pushed to the sides as a bass moves up to strike."

On the Delta, which offers the traditional style of mat fishing, Barrack monitors the tides so he can stay with water levels where bass are most aggressive. By doing so, he can fish the frog at a more moderate pace without being forced to slow his retrieves.

Unlike other bass fishing disciplines, strike de-

tection with frogs is hardly a subtle affair. Instead, the sudden explosion of bass and grass often spells trouble for novice mat maestros who haven't dialed down their heart rate.

"Fishing the bait with the rod held high, in the 2 o'clock position, is extremely important," counsels Thomas. "When the fish blows up on the bait, your first instinct is to jerk.

"The correct response is to drop your rod tip and point it directly at the lure and take up slack as you would in preparing for a worm strike. The fish will usually meet you halfway, tightening up the line as you do the same."

Pointing the rod toward the fish gives it a chance to take the bait and turn. At the same time, you're lowering the rod into a better position for the hook set.

With so much riding on a delayed hook set, Barrack, Munk and Thomas all rely on 20-pound monofilament instead of the less-forgiving braided lines. They also agree that the proper rod action is medium/heavy to heavy.

Whatever tackle one uses and wherever the summer mats, tules or grassbeds beckon, an angler should forget the downside of the so-called "dog days" of summer and remember that when the big ones start busting through the mats, the world suddenly seems air-conditioned.

WATER WILLOW and similar emergent weeds can be difficult to fish effectively with anything but a surface frog. Pros aim their casts past openings in the vegetation and crawl and hop the lures over the weeds and through the holes. When a bass strikes a frog, it's crucial to pause a second or two before setting the hook — to ensure the fish has the lure solidly in its mouth.

MAKING THE MOST OF BUZZBAITS

Spring through fall, no other lure brings more exciting strikes

THE BUZZBAIT is a ridiculous-looking lure. Aside from the way it skitters on the surface like a vulnerable creature trying to escape, its basic appearance offers little semblance to a natural aquatic animal.

Texas angler Mike Dyess says it best: "I think bass look at a buzzbait about the same way people judge airline food: They don't know what it is, but they eat it anyway."

That was especially true in the early days when an angler could throw just about any kind of sur-

face churning blade around cover and catch fish all day. But on today's heavily fished lakes, educated bass aren't as likely to blast foolishly at anything that sputters by.

But that doesn't mean the buzzbait doesn't deserve a special spot in the tacklebox. To the contrary, it remains one of the pros' favorite weapons for catching big bass under the right conditions.

"I have a box of buzzbaits that never leave my boat and are always in the back of my mind," says three time B.A.S.S. Angler of the Year Kevin

VanDam. "When conditions are right, you can use the buzzbait to catch the biggest stringer of your life."

Of course, choosing the right conditions isn't always foolproof. But even when the bass aren't inhaling buzzbaits, the experts have learned how to refine their presentations and have devised little tricks that help them select and use buzzbaits more efficiently.

WHEN TO USE THEM

Arkansas pro Rob Kilby believes there really isn't a bad time to throw a buzzbait. While the prime time is from the postspawn through the fall, Kilby has caught buzzbait bass as early as March and as late as December.

Nor is it only an early morning or late evening lure. Pros say some of the biggest bass of their lives were caught on buzzbaits between 11 a.m. and

2 p.m., when other anglers opt for slower finesse presentations.

Weather does seem to play a role, with stable conditions tending to produce the best buzzbait bites. But Kilby swears there's no better lure to fish during a steady rain. And Rick Clunn had one of his best buzzbait days during a snowstorm in Tennessee years ago.

"It was one of those real quiet snows that seemed to muffle

BUZZBAITS ARE the ultimate reaction baits. The overhead delta buzz blade churns the water, drawing bass to the pulsing skirt and baitfishlike head. Late spring is a prime time for buzzers, but the lures will catch fish almost year-round.

A Dozen Buzzin' Tips

1. To keep a buzzbait from tumbling and tangling on the cast, leave 18 inches of line between the lure and the rod tip.
2. Heavy line prevents breakoffs in thick cover, and it helps keep the lure riding high on the surface.
3. Maintaining the proper speed requires concentration. In most cases, listen for a steady plop-plop-plop cadence.
4. The squeak of a buzz blade rotating on the wire seems to draw more strikes. To increase the noise, crimp the rivet at the end of the blade.
5. Tie a buzzbait to your car's radio antenna as you drive down the highway to "tune" the blade.
6. For easier casting of 1/4-ounce and smaller buzzbaits, mash some split shot onto the hook shank.
7. Superlines, either fluorocarbon or braided lines, will aid in hook sets.
8. Prime time for throwing a buzzbait is warm weather just prior to passage of a cold front.
9. Always keep a "comeback lure" — a worm, grub or soft jerkbait — handy when fishing a buzzbait. If a bass misses the buzzer, throw into the same area with the slow sinking backup bait.
10. Like most lures, buzzbaits come in a variety of colors. You can cover all the bases with white for bright days and black for dark skies.
11. Cast beyond your target, and you'll get surer strikes. Tournaments have been won by anglers casting buzzbaits onto the bank and dragging them into the water.
12. To prevent short strikes, trim the skirt to a point even with the belly of the hook.

BASS ARE notorious for striking buzzbaits and missing the hooks. For extra strike insurance, add a trailer hook to the main blade. Use a single stinger where the cover is thick, and a treble trailer hook in open water.

every other sound," Clunn recalls. "The seemingly irrational thought entered my mind that I should throw a buzzbait, so I picked it up, and the results were awesome. The only sound you could hear was the buzzbait coming across the surface — until the bass exploded on it. They weren't nibbling it, either. They swallowed it."

Most pros agree that those bluebird days following a cold front may be the worst time to try buzzbaiting, but don't rule them out, either.

"It can be especially effective if there's a good chop on the water," says VanDam. "One day on Lake Fork (Texas), I was catching 4- to 7-pounders in the middle of a bright, sunny day on a 1/2-ounce buzzbait that I bounced across the waves. It must have looked like shad skipping over the surface, because the bass were crushing it."

CHOOSING A LURE

Buzzbaits come in a variety of sizes, shapes and configurations, with the in-line buzzer and safety-pin style being the most popular. The in-line buzzer is best suited for fishing fast through sparse grass and lily pads, while the safety-pin style (hook rides beneath the surface while the blade churns on top) is the most popular for fishing around open water or wood.

The traditional buzzbait can be dressed with multiple blades, multiple "wings" on the blades, and with holes in the blades to create additional commotion and a bubble trail behind the lure.

Arizona pro Dean Rojas likes buzzbaits with multiple wings — single blades with more than two bent ears — for slowing the bait down on short casts.

"When I'm making short pitches to targets and want the bait to come up fast, I use the triple- or quadruple-wing buzzbaits," he says. "They allow me to make soft presentations at specific targets nearby."

Blade materials vary, too, but the aluminum blade is widely preferred for several reasons. The ears on the blade can be bent slightly to change its speed or alter running angle. More important, aluminum makes more noise.

But aluminum is not always best, says Rojas.

"There are times when the flash coming off the aluminum blade can be a deterrent in clear water," he explains. "The plastic blade gives you the same surface commotion and a lit-

tle reflection. I may match it with a black skirt so that all the fish see is the commotion and a black image."

Aluminum blades, however, tend to produce more of a squeaky sound than plastic blades, and many anglers believe the squeak is as important to the bait's appeal as is its sputtering.

Therefore, says Clunn, noise is especially important in stained or muddy water.

Some buzzbaits have squeaks built into them, but most pros customize their lures to squeal even more. Years ago, this was done by holding the buzzbait out the vehicle window as the angler drove to the lake, to make the blade wear on the wire as it turned in the wind.

A simpler solution is to remove the blade and pop the rivet from the wire shaft, sandpaper the wire to ensure all the paint is removed, then replace the blade and rivet.

Some buzzbaits are clackers, meaning they have a metal tab that clanks against the blade or the wire shaft to create additional noise. Most pros contend the clacking isn't necessary unless you're fishing heavily stained water or trying to draw bass from a deep grassbed.

SLOWER IS BETTER

Ask most pros about their favorite buzzbait presentations and the majority will tell you, "The slower, the better."

"Most people fish a buzzbait way too fast," says Kilby. "Slowing the bait keeps it in the strike zone longer and gets you more strikes."

You can fish it slower by reducing lure size, using lures with multiple blades or wings, or by bending the wings slightly outward.

Kilby's favorite size is 1/4 ounce, which he says gets more strikes, especially when fishing is slow.

Unfortunately, smaller buzzbaits can be a bugger to cast in the wind or for long distances. To compensate, Rick Clunn clamps a small rubber core sinker on the hook shaft of a 1/4- or 3/8-ounce Lunker Lure just below the head. This not only adds casting weight, but it also helps keep the head directly below the blade.

Swindle prefers bigger baits, so he achieves a slower speed by replacing the blade on a 3/8-ounce buzzbait with the larger blade that comes on the 1/2-ounce model. He also adds a trailer to the rear hook, which adds buoyancy.

Color is often debated, but most pros seem little concerned about the color of the skirt on their buzzbaits. White and shad colors are preferred for bright days, and dark colors on cloudy days. Translucent skirts can be good in ultraclear water.

"I tell fishermen to start with no skirt at all, especially on windy days when the skirt can hamper your casts," says Zell Rowland. "The fish will let you know what they want."

The skirtless buzzer is a theory shared by Dyess, who credits Clunn with helping him catch fish during a tournament on Lake Mead.

"Bass can be fussy about stuff like that, even with a buzzbait," he says. "It's a lure that deserves attention to detail, just like any other bait in your tacklebox."

WHEN BASS are in thick cover, a buzzbait will attract their attention, but it must be placed fairly close to the strike zone to get them to move. Whenever possible, bump the lure into brush, stumps and trees; the erratic movement that ensues often triggers a bite.

In-line Buzzers

The original Floyd's Buzzer, which is still being made, is one of the pros' favorites for fishing fast through sparse grass and around lily pads. The teardrop blade and wire weedguard make the in-line extremely snag resistant. Traditional safety pin-style buzzbaits will work around vegetation, too, but their main strength is in fishing around wood cover.

U

UNDERWATER PLUGS

Chunk and wind.
Stop and go.
You provide the action
with these bass baits . . .

HIT 'EM WITH CRANKBAITS

You'll get more hits from bass if the lure hits something first

MIKE AUTEN has been a dedicated cranker ever since he caught his first bass on a diving bait.

"I had marked a ledge where it dropped from 8 to 20 feet, just like I'd read about in the maga-zines," Auten remembers. "Then I just started casting and cranking. On one cast, the lure hit a stump and seemed to shoot off at an angle just for an instant, and I felt it start to roll through the water like it was on its side — the normal retrieve

"But no matter when or where you use them, the key is *deflection* — hitting cover or structure with the lure and triggering a reaction strike. It's something I try for on every cast."

Bass fishermen have long recognized this, but Auten's analysis goes a step farther. "If you watch a school of shad swim, every once in a while the light hits one a certain way and that fish just flashes for a second," he explains. "It catches your eye immediately because it's different, even if you're not paying that much attention.

"When a crankbait hits something and deflects away, it turns on its side momentarily. I think it causes this same visual effect for any nearby bass. The lure's action suddenly changes. It flashes, and that's what triggers the bass into striking."

Veteran pro Guy Eaker adds, "That's why depth is your primary consideration when choosing a crankbait. You have to be able to get the lure deep enough to hit bottom or bottom cover. Each crankbait is designed to reach a certain depth, so to be able to fish them year-round on different cover and structure, a fisherman will need a variety of crankbaits in his tacklebox.

Wood Vs. Plastic Crankbaits

One of the most often-asked questions concerning crankbait fishing is whether to choose a lure made from wood or from plastic. Manufacturers and fishermen disagree on the answer.

Dieter Stanford, maker of flat-sided cedar crankbaits, feels that well-built wood cranks are generally more reliable and consistent than plastic baits. "They tend to run true out of the box," Stanford believes. Wood baits are also a little heavier than plastic versions, making long casts easier.

Peter Allen, maker of plastic crankbaits, thinks the benefits of plastic lures outweigh those of wood. "You can fill plastic baits with rattles, so they are louder than wood. You can also achieve near-neutral buoyancy with plastic — something impossible to do with wood," Allen continues.

resistance wasn't there. Then something hit it so hard I nearly lost my rod.

"It was a bass that weighed 6 1/2 pounds, and believe me, for someone who grew up fishing an old strip-mining pit in Indiana, that was a big bass."

Without realizing it at the time, Auten, one of the rising stars on the CITGO BASSMASTER Tournament Trail, discovered what he today considers one of the basics of crankbait fishing.

"Crankbaits can be fished year-round," he says.

"Some manufacturers print depth information for their crankbaits on each package, but this is only for use as a general guideline," he continues. "You can vary the depth a crankbait runs by changing your line size, slowing or speeding up your retrieve, holding your rod tip up or down, and making longer or shorter casts.

"Just about the only time you don't want a crankbait to hit the bottom is when you're fishing over submerged vegetation, or when you know the bass are suspended," Eaker says. "When you're fishing over vegetation, you want to keep your lure just above the grass, and when the fish are suspended, you try to get your crankbait running right through them, not under or above them."

CRANKBAITS WORK in any season. One key is matching a lure's diving depth to the depth at which bass are feeding.

BILL MAKES A DIFFERENCE

In part, the length of a crankbait's bill, as well as the angle of that bill, determines the depth a lure will dive. Shallow diving crankbaits have bills that angle downward at about 30 degrees, while deeper divers have straight bills.

"The primary depth I fish with a crankbait throughout the year is 10 feet or less," says Auten. "The deepest I've ever fished a crankbait is about 14 feet. I know a number of crankbaits are advertised as being able to reach 20 feet or even deeper, but I've never fished one that deep. If bass are below 15 feet, I change to a vertical presentation with another lure that I believe is more efficient at that depth."

Adds Eaker, "Fishermen have to evaluate their own efficiency when they start fishing deeper than 15 feet or so. In many instances, vertical presentations are more accurate. The deeper you fish a crankbait, the longer you have to cast — it takes longer for the bait to reach bottom. Going deeper usually requires a longer rod as well as lighter line.

"There's a lot of difference between cranking at 10 feet and cranking at 20 feet."

A crankbait's bill also helps determine the lure's action, as does the "pull point," or line-tie location. Bills that angle down create a wider side-to-side motion (called "wobble"), and a line tie farther out on the bill has a similar effect. Conversely, crankbaits with straight bills tend to have a tighter wobble, as do crankbaits on which the line tie is located closer to the body or even on the nose of the lure.

"When I'm fishing 5 feet or less, I generally want a crankbait with a wider wobble, so I choose a lure with the bill angled down," says Auten. "At this depth, I'm fishing visible cover in stained water, so the wider wobble displaces more water and the bass can find the lure easier.

"A crankbait with a wider wobble can also be worked slower without losing its action. That's why it's a good lure choice in early spring, when the water is still cold. When you fish a tight-wobbling crankbait slowly, it loses its action."

Since too much vibration may actually discourage fish from striking, tight-wobbling crankbaits usually are preferred in clear water.

The deeper you fish a crankbait — as may be necessary in summer — the tighter the wobble you want; in fact, the majority of really deep diving crankbaits made today have a tight wobble. That's because wide-wobbling crankbaits produce so much vibration at depth, they're difficult and inefficient to use; their vibration is so strong you can't feel a fish strike.

Many believe the body design of a crankbait also determines its action, but this is only partly true. The different body shapes do disperse water differently to produce slightly different sounds, but this is more noticeable to fish than to fishermen.

"In truth, you can alter any crankbait's action simply by changing the line-tie location," explains Auten. "Manufacturers can make a flat-sided lure do anything a rounded crankbait can do, and vice versa.

"Manufacturers match the bill angle with the line-tie location to achieve a desired action and depth. That's one reason similar-looking crankbaits from different companies have completely different actions."

SUSPENDERS FOR BASS

When bass are holding tight to cover and seem reluctant to chase lures, making a crankbait stop and hover teasingly beside that cover may help generate strikes. The lures that do this are known as "suspending" crankbaits, and several manufacturers have them in their lineups. Others add one or more of the stick-on SuspenDots manufactured by Storm to gain additional weight.

Some pros, such as Eaker, even have developed a special technique known as "stand-still" crankbaiting that keeps the lure suspending beside the cover almost indefinitely.

"As soon as I feel the crankbait hit the cover, I stop reeling," explains Eaker. "This lets the crankbait begin to float away, and after a pause I start reeling again, or simply pull the lure back into the cover with my rod tip. When I feel it hit, I stop so the lure can start floating back again. You can keep this up as long as you want to, and the lure will only move a few inches each time."

This is often a good technique in colder weather when fish are usually less active. In the winter months, Auten prefers to work his crankbaits parallel to steep or vertical banks and rock riprap. Depending on water clarity, he uses a medium diver and 12- to 14-pound-test line to work depths between 6 and about 8 feet.

"In the winter, I really try to target multiple cover/structure locations," the Kentucky pro explains. "I really like stumps along the edge of a creek channel, or maybe a pile of broken rocks along a bluff. You always increase your chances when you can find places like this, but in winter, this type of cover often helps keep bass in a little shallower water."

Auten and Eaker both like to use crankbaits during the prespawn season and again after the spawn. Such baits, however, aren't the most efficient to use when bass are on beds.

"In prespawn, I like to fish extremely shallow cover, again with stumps if I can find them," says Auten. "For the most part, I'm looking for individual fish in protected areas, so I use a shallow run-

ning crankbait that covers water from 1 to 3 feet. Because bass using that cover are likely to be heavy ones, I'll also fish 14- to 20-pound-test line."

In the postspawn, Eaker advises fishing secondary structure, such as the first available cover or depth changes away from spawning flats, including creek points and deeper grasslines. Medium running crankbaits that cover the range between 5 and 10 feet are his choices.

In summer, Auten and Eaker fish deeper crankbaits 10 to 14 feet over channel breaks, sunken roadbeds and main lake points, while in autumn, both anglers key on shallow cover less than 5 feet deep and any places with current in the backs of tributary creeks.

COLOR CHOICES

"As always, baitfish are important in fall creek patterns," says Auten. "At that time of year, I really try to use crankbaits that look like shad. Silver/blue back is a favorite color that produces well for me, along with silver/black back.

"In spring, I'll often use a red crankbait to try to imitate crawfish, while in stained or muddy water, I like chartreuse/blue or chartreuse/black back because I think the bass can see chartreuse better.

"These are just my preferences, and I readily admit I'm not at all sure how important they are to bass. During a bass tournament on Alabama's Lake Martin, the top three positions were won using the same model crankbait, but in three different colors," Auten notes.

"It's important for a fisherman to keep shallow, medium and deep diving crankbaits in his favorite colors, because then he'll be ready for year-round action."

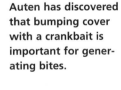

PRO ANGLER Mike Auten has discovered that bumping cover with a crankbait is important for generating bites.

WITH A MOUTHFUL of tiny, sharp trebles, an energetic largemouth is a challenge to land by hand.

FINESSE CRANKBAITS FOR TOUGH TIMES

Casting these midget plugs is an adventure

MIDGET CRANKBAITS get little respect from tournament competitors who are seeking heavyweight bass. Larger lures cast better, routinely produce bigger fish and wield capable hooks that let you assert some degree of authority over rambunctious bass.

With bantam crankbaits weighing less than 1/4 ounce, every cast is an adventure. Pinpoint accuracy goes out the window, and those bitty treble hooks

one of Ohio's most celebrated tournament anglers. "The mini Big-O has been one of my bread-and-butter lures for years."

The littlest Big-O is lighter than its listed weight of 1/4 ounce and qualifies as a true finesse crankbait. Polosky replaces the original hooks with slightly oversize Gamakatsu trebles, and claims that they significantly reduce the number of fish he loses. He flings the little crankbait with a light action, 6-foot rod and 8-pound line.

"I do especially well with the Big-O right after the spawn, when you begin seeing bass fry," says Polosky. "It also works well when the shad are small, usually in midsummer or later. Actually, I've caught bass with that bait from early spring to late fall."

In shallow water situations, where finesse crankbaits serve best, Polosky runs the Big-O past fallen trees, stumps, boat docks, weeds — essentially the same cover he fishes with larger lures.

"It swims over cover real well," he says. "The slower you crank it, the fewer fish you'll lose. That lets bass come up behind it and suck it in and get the hooks in the soft part of their mouths."

EASY DOES IT

After a bass has engulfed the crankbait, light rod pressure is essential to prevent ripping out the little treble hooks. When the bass runs, pay out line or suffer the consequences.

SMALL AND almost weightless, downsized crankbaits and lipless crankbaits like these are easier to cast on light line and spinning gear.

don't exactly instill confidence that you'll ever land a sizable bass.

So why put up with the frustration? Because finesse crankbaits consistently draw more strikes than "bubba" baits. While it's true that many fish caught on small crankbaits will be undersize throwbacks, some will pass the minimum length mark on measuring boards, including an occasional lunker. When bass refuse to bite in tournaments, these little lures can eke out enough fish to earn a payday.

"I can't tell you how many times tiny crankbaits have come through for me," says George Polosky,

TINY BASS PLUGS like these are great for fishing in streams, ponds and other small waters. They're also excellent cures when reservoir bass get "lockjaw."

NOT MANY PROS are willing to endure the frustration of fishing midget crankbaits. Harold Allen is an exception.

Loosening the drag may do this, but Polosky prefers to tighten his drag, switch off the anti-reverse and backreel.

"I always backreel," he says. "You've got to be patient and play them out. It drives you nuts, but I've landed 5-pound bass with that little thing."

Zell Rowland, one of the few touring pros on the B.A.S.S. circuit who counts on finesse crankbaits, improves his catch rate with these lures by sharpening the hooks with a small file.

"People wonder how I land bass with such little hooks," says Rowland, "but it's not as hard as you think. A bass usually gets these baits well back in its mouth, and sharpened hooks latch on everywhere. The fish can't get rid of it easily."

During a B.A.S.S. tournament on New York's St. Lawrence River, the tiny trebles on a 1/10-ounce Rebel Crickhopper helped Rowland reel in a limit of smallmouth bass that weighed nearly 14 pounds.

He had switched from a jerkbait to the Crickhopper because several other competitors were working over his fishing area. The previous day, everyone had scored well on jerkbaits. On the second day, however, the bass systematically refused jerkbaits and other traditional smallmouth offerings. It seemed as though they had vanished.

Rowland eventually resorted to an ultralight spinning rod with 4-pound line and began slinging the Crickhopper. While other anglers around him continued to struggle, Rowland landed nearly 75 smallmouth weighing up to 3 1/2 pounds. It was not the first (or the last) time finesse crankbaits saved the day for him.

"I don't go anywhere in the United States without a little bitty box with several of these lures in different colors," he says. Along with Crickhoppers, Rowland's assortment includes Rebel's Creek Creature, Hellgrammite and Teeny Wee-Crawfish and Cordell's 1/8-ounce Spot Minnow. He custom-paints some of these lures with yellow hues to match the color of mayflies when they hatch in the spring. Finesse crankbaits produce especially well for Rowland after the bass spawn, and also through the summer.

With the exception of sinking, vibrating crankbaits, such as the 1/8-ounce Tiny Trap from Bill Lewis Lures and the Cordell Spot Minnow, most finesse crankbaits are floater-divers that run only 2 to 4 feet deep. They're at their best around shallow, visible cover. For the most part, you fish them just as you would conventional crankbaits in the same circumstances.

"Other than downsizing to ultralight tackle," says Rowland, "there is little difference in fishing a little crankbait compared to a regular crankbait. Just remember that small crankbaits have a tendency to roll at high speeds."

CLEAR ADVANTAGE

Although finesse crankbaits do catch bass in stained water, these subtle lures perform best in clear water, where bass feed mainly by sight. Bass pro Harold Allen discovered this years ago while fishing an early spring tournament on Lake Bistineau, La.

During practice, Allen had located a good bunch of fish in a cove that held exceptionally clear water. He had little trouble catching them on spinnerbaits and plastic worms, and he felt confident the area would help him score well in the tournament.

His confidence waned the next morning when he discovered that a severe cold front had assaulted the region overnight. The air temperature had dropped so drastically that the water along the shoreline had become a rim of ice.

"When I got to my fishing hole," recalls Allen, "I could see bass cruising around just under the surface. I threw just about everything I had at them, even 4-inch worms, but they didn't show the slightest interest in anything."

As a last resort, Allen tied on a Rebel Super Tiny R. Before the day was over, the finesse crankbait duped a respectable mess of bass and prevented Allen from bombing out, as many of his competitors did that day.

"I'd crank that thing along just beneath the surface," says Allen, "and the water was so clear I could actually watch the bass slowly swim up behind the lure and suck it in."

While most anglers opt for spinning tackle when fishing with finesse crankbaits, Allen steadfastly clings to baitcasting gear. He backs off the anti-backlash mechanism on his reel so the spool gives line freely, and he relies on his thumb to prevent overruns. It takes a great degree of skill and practice, but he manages quite well with a light action graphite rod and 8-pound-test line. Allen also relies on his educated thumb when fighting bass.

"When a bass stops me cold," says Allen, "I immediately push the spool release on my reel. If it hits with a burst of speed, I can let it run and not rely on my drag. When it stops, I click the reel in gear and get back whatever line I can.

"Apply light pressure. The more you pressure them, the harder they fight."

HOOKED ON FISHING

The most endearing feature of finesse crankbaits is their ability to produce a lot of strikes, especially when getting youngsters hooked on fishing.

"They're the greatest baits ever made for taking a kid pond fishing," says Rowland. "Give a youngster a pushbutton outfit with 4- or 6-pound line and a Hellgrammite — that's probably the best crankbait for ponds — and he'll catch everything from bass to bluegill to whatever swims in that pond."

Small streams provide another superb option for finesse crankbaits, whether you are introducing kids to fishing or just out to get away from it all and catch a bunch of fish. Lisa Hughes

VETERAN PRO Harold Allen fishes finesse crankbaits with light baitcasting tackle and casts them to visible cover in shallow water.

dotes on stream fishing with lures of this type.

Hughes has fished streams across the country from the bank, while wade fishing and from inner tube floats. The 6-pound line on her ultralight spinning outfit usually sports a Crickhopper or a Teeny Wee-Crawfish.

"On one outing," she says, "I was tube fishing in a river. Nobody was doing any good, but my little crankbait caught a smallmouth, a largemouth, a rock bass, a bluegill and a catfish. They were small fish, but I get a kick out of catching a variety of species."

Besides, even with finesse crankbaits, there's always the chance that a big one will strike. Just ask Hughes. On one of her stream fishing excursions, she landed a largemouth that weighed nearly 8 pounds — on a Creek Creature.

Relatively few bass tournament anglers will ever put much stock in finesse crankbaits — despite their effectiveness. But these lures certainly deserve what little space they take up in your tacklebox.

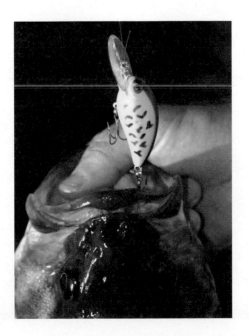

QUARTER-OUNCE crankbaits, like this medium running plug, have their places in a bass angler's arsenal.

DEEP CRANKING FOR PAIN AND PROFIT

Drag up bass with a diving bait

(Opposite page) BILL DANCE uses a suspending lure in a technique he calls "worming" a crankbait. After cranking it to the bottom, he pulls it with the rod as if he were scooting a plastic worm along the bottom.

DURING THE LAST TWO DECADES OR SO, the brightest minds in the world of bass fishing have managed to develop a precious few lures that went on to have a radical impact on our sport.

One of those revolutionary lures was Mann's Deep 20+, a crankbait that ushered in the ultradeep cranking craze that swept the late 1980s.

Since the 1986 introduction of that groundbreaking creation by the late Jack Davis, nearly every major lure manufacturer has developed a maximum-depth plug. As a result of the high-profile tournament successes of pros like David Fritts, Rick Clunn and Paul Elias, these deep divers have commanded a role in our everyday fishing lives.

In some ways, that has been a mixed blessing.

The superdeep crankbait opened up a new arena, allowing crankers to go where only trolled and bottom-hugging baits had ever gone before. But in the months that followed their arrival, many fishermen were quickly discouraged by the physical demands involved in pulling these big divers through their deepest runs. And some anglers became disenchanted with the exaggerated claims that driving these oversized plugs down to their optimum depth was a breeze. In truth, deep cranking is anything but easy. There is a definite art to ultradeep cranking.

DEEP DIVING CRANKBAITS — distinguished by their oversize lips — have made the key bass depth range of 15 to 20 feet attainable by search lures.

THE UPSIDE

"The advent of baits like the Mann's 20+ has done wonders for this sport," says Elias. "In the places where you could only fish a worm before, now you can get there with a crankbait.

"And when you can get a crankbait down to cover in 15 to 20 feet, you can do some damage, because these are places where the bass are not accustomed to seeing a bait swim quickly by. They will react to it every time."

"For finding fish in that 15- to 20-foot range, it is one of the best tools available," adds Louisiana pro John Torian. "These are the fish that rarely got tapped in tournaments before these crankbaits came along."

Tricks For Reaching Maximum Depths

Here are a few pro tricks for gaining a little added depth from superdeep crankbaits:

KNEEL-AND-REEL — Paul Elias made it fashionable to fish on your knees with the top 2 feet of the rod thrust under water when he won the 1982 BASS Masters Classic with a Norman Deep N crankbait. The later development of ultradeep crankbaits eliminated much of the need to kneel-and-reel, but today's most knowledgeable crankers still resort to this old tactic from time to time.

"I'm not a big believer in kneeling-and-reeling, but there are situations where I will stick my rod tip into the water to get the few extra inches necessary to hit a stump or rock," David Fritts advises. "A lot of times sticking the tip of your rod in the water will allow that bait to go an extra 8 inches to 18 inches deeper. It also helps reduce the bow (slack) in your line."

WEIGHTING A CRANKBAIT — Fritts made weighting big-lip crankbaits famous en route to winning the 1993 Classic. In those days, he drilled Poe's wooden crankbaits and inserted melted lead in strategic spots to achieve neutral buoyancy in the baits, enabling them to reach the deepest structure — as well as suspend in front of inactive bass.

Today, he takes an easier approach: He simply applies several Storm SuspenDots or SuspenStrips (small, self-adhesive lead patches that enable fishermen to fine-tune the weighting process easily) to the body and/or throat of his lures.

Not all crankbaits are created equal — not even when made by the same company. Over the years, Fritts has learned that one version of a certain wooden or plastic crankbait will run a foot or so deeper than another bait of the same make and model. He scratches the bill of these baits to indicate which are his best deep swimmers.

THE FINE-TUNING PROCESS — Only a perfectly running crankbait is capable of reaching its maximum depth. A lure that veers a foot or so during retrieve can "cost you a couple of feet of depth," according to Michigan pro Kevin VanDam. "It's critical that the crankbait run straight."

Correcting the problem — called tuning — is easy. To tune a crankbait, use pliers to slightly bend the eye of the lure in the opposite direction from the way it has been running. For example, if it tracks too far to the left, turn the eye to the right.

SHAVING DEPTH — "There have been instances where I've won tournaments by filing down the bill of crankbaits," Fritts states. "I just take a file and file down the very bottom of the leading edge of the bill until that edge is real sharp. This makes the bill so sharp that it cuts through the water differently, makes a different sound and runs a little deeper.

"It makes the lure dig a little harder or dig a little deeper because it is like a knife cutting the water versus bringing your hand through the water.

"Not many people do this, but it is a little trick that can pay off big at times. The bait is only going to last a day or two, though, because the bill is going to wear down eventually."

BILL DANCE CRANKS a bend in a creek channel — a piece of deep structure for which a deep diving crankbait is perfectly suited.

Michigan's Kevin VanDam, who has developed a reputation as a superb *power* fisherman, touts the deepest of diving baits. But he emphasizes that we shouldn't get completely caught up in the race to reach the deepest bass of all.

"I've really experimented with about every type of crankbait out there — especially the deep diving ones — to see how deep I can get them and what they do once they reach the bottom," the two time B.A.S.S. Angler of the Year relates. "And I feel like 17 feet is about the maximum depth I can consistently get a bait down, hit the bottom and feel comfortable and confident that I'm working the lure properly to catch the fish that are there.

"Fifteen feet and less is where I still spend 99 percent of my time fishing. There are crankbaits like a Mann's 30+ and (Bomber's) Fat Free Shad that will get down deeper than that, but I just haven't developed a lot of confidence in a great big lure much deeper than 15 feet, and I seem to lose a lot of fish that deep. The value of a real deep diver like a Fat Free Shad, to me, is being able

to dig up the bottom in water that is a little shallower than the bait's maximum depth."

"There are only a few crankbaits out there that actually do run in the 15-foot range, and even fewer that go a little deeper," adds Bill Dance, another two time Angler of the Year.

THE DOWNSIDE

"A lot of people are good at cranking shallow cover," Fritts reminds us. "But deep cranking is a whole different story."

Much of the initial disappointment with these hard-charging superdeep crankers centers around the initial claims of some lure makers that overcoming the seemingly magical 20-foot barrier was a simple matter. At least one manufacturer alleged that an average cast with almost any rod and a medium retrieve was enough to get its product to dive to such levels.

Most serious bass fishermen have learned by now that the truth is several fathoms away from such claims.

"Reaching 20 feet is not easy," Roland Martin says emphatically. "There is a misconception that you can tie one of these new superdeep crankbaits on 15-pound-test line, make a normal cast with a 5 1/2-foot rod and reach 20 feet. But you couldn't get the best of these superdeep divers

below 15 feet under those circumstances.

"A lot of people bought into that myth. They thought that just because they went out and spent $5 for that crankbait, it would run down to 20 feet. They found out that it's simply not true."

"With ultradeep cranking, you have to understand a few basic laws of physics," Dance says. "There are five requirements for extra-deep cranking — a long cast, a long rod, light line, the proper lure and the right speed of retrieve. You cannot get around those things."

Even Fritts readily admits that piloting a crankbait near the 20-foot zone isn't "automatic" for him. The North Carolina pro also acknowledges that the physical strain involved in

WHILE OTHER ANGLERS are burning up the bank, savvy fishermen probe deeper flats with a fast moving, deep diving crankbait. Fish receive little pressure in these staging areas.

LEARN PRECISELY how deep each bait in your box runs, and match it to the depth bass are holding. At times, a deep runner can be deadly in shallow water as it dredges the bottom and churns up a silt trail.

propelling these wide-bodied, magnum-lipped baits through the water is so great that he prefers to sit while cranking. In this position, the rod rests against his leg and absorbs some of the punishment usually endured by the arms and hands.

"Deep cranking is not for everybody," Elias advises. "Throwing these big-lip crankbaits and powering them back to the boat over and over is the most physically taxing technique in bass fishing."

TACKLE CONSIDERATIONS

No technique demands such a balanced harmony of tackle — or puts as much strain on equipment — as deep cranking.

Cranking experts beef up their tackle for probing the deepest bass lairs. For most, that begins with a flexible 7- or 7 1/2-foot rod, knowing that the extra length significantly enhances casting distance — the most critical element in enabling a crankbait to do its designed job. The additional rod length also provides more long-distance hook-

MANY PROS FISH crankbaits on limber rods made of fiberglass or composite materials. The extra flex makes it easier for the angler to set the hook and harder for the fish to throw the lure.

setting power, as well as a little extra depth by cranking with the tip section below the surface.

When crankbaiting deep structure, Fritts pegs his average cast at about 40 yards (with an occasional 50-yard toss).

Many fishermen have followed Rick Clunn's lead by cranking with fiberglass (or composite) rods, which are less sensitive than graphite. According to a popular theory, the deadened sensitivity slightly delays an angler's hook setting response, which gives a bass more time to inhale a fast moving lure. With graphite rods, some believe there is a tendency to react so quickly that the crankbait can actually be taken away from the fish.

(Other skilled crankers favor the sensitivity of graphite, which enables them to feel bottom cover, structure and fish. Anglers would be well-advised to try each, to see which works best for them.)

The high-speed reels so popular for fishing jigs and soft plastics are not well-suited for superdeep

cranking. The better crankbaiters stick with lightweight, medium-speed models with gear ratios ranging from 3.8:1 to 5.1:1.

Line size, particularly its diameter, is a primary consideration when attempting to milk every inch of depth from a diving bait. Lighter line simply provides more depth by reducing the amount of inches-robbing friction that occurs as it is dragged through the water.

"By switching from regular 17-pound monofilament to 10-pound, which has a much smaller diameter, I can get a Norman DD22 to run almost 2 feet deeper," says Larry Lazoen, an eight time Classic qualifier. "And that can make a big difference."

Fritts believes that the amount of resistance created by a reel's drag system can also translate into a few less inches of depth. For that reason, he uses the smoothest drag available and relies on its lowest setting.

CASTING DISTANCE

In this case, the amount of line that goes out determines how far down any crankbait will run. Dance calls it "basic geometry."

"The length of your cast is everything," explains the television show star. Dance helped develop the Fat Free Shad, which won the 1995 Classic in its first month on the market. "Your lure will simply dive much deeper on a 40-foot cast than it will on a 20-foot cast. That is because the lure has enough line out to be able to stay down at its maximum depth longer.

"The longer cast gives you better depth control. There are also drawbacks to long casting. For one thing, you don't have nearly as much hook setting power, and you can't feel your lure as well as you can at close range because of line stretch."

THE RIGHT RETRIEVE

Feeling the need for speed? Ignore it if you hope to get a deep diver down to its peak level.

Overpowering or burning a crankbait actually hinders its diving ability. Lazoen echoes the sentiments of other top fishermen when he emphasizes that the key to a bait reaching its maximum depth is a slow to moderate retrieval speed. For a crankbait to gain its greatest depth, water must deflect evenly off each side of its strategically designed lip, which serves as a diving plane. Cranking too fast can cause water to flow off the front of the lip and significantly increase friction.

Most anglers know that water temperature controls the activity levels of bass and dictates retrieval speed. "As silly as this might sound, water temperature also affects the running depth of a lure," Dance interjects. "Cold water is much denser than warm water. In other words, the colder water gets, the thicker it becomes. The warmer water gets, the thinner it becomes.

"This means you will get better depth control in 80 degree water than you will in 60 degree water. This 20 degree difference in temperature may only cause your bait to run a foot or so deeper or shallower, but that little difference can have a major impact on whether you catch bass."

And when it comes to gaining a foothold in a world where fast moving lures have never gone before, mere inches are what separates the most consistently successful crankbait fishermen from the rest of the angling crowd.

GETTING THE MOST FROM LIPLESS CRANKBAITS

There's more to fishing noisy crankbaits than meets the ear

SOME MIGHT SAY that an angler earns his degree in lipless crankbait fishing the moment he completes his first cast.

Cast. Crank. Cast. Crank. Burn the bait over shallow water and wait for an irritated bass to slam it like a freight train. That's all you really need to know to catch bass on one of the most simplistic, yet reliable bass catchers known to man.

But B.A.S.S. pros rarely settle for the simple approach. When a bait draws as many strikes and catches as many fish as does the lipless crankbait, serious anglers find multiple ways to employ it.

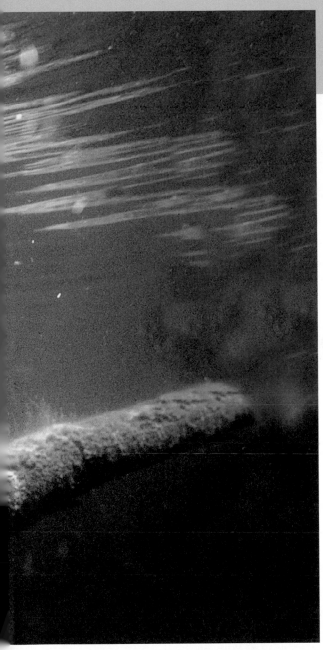

Read Your Lipless
Not all lipless crankbaits are created equal. Make sure you know the traits of the bait you are throwing:
— Does it sink head first or horizontally?
— Is the wobble wide or tight?
— Is the rattle obnoxious or subdued?

"I haven't caught a fish by straight reeling a lipless lure for three years," says Florida pro Terry Seagraves. "The traditional presentation of continuous cranking catches fish, but that's not always the best way to work one of these lures."

Missouri pro Randy Blaukat says there really isn't a "best" way to fish a lipless lure without first letting the fish tell you how they want it.

"It's a far more versatile bait than most anglers realize," says Blaukat. "You've got to experiment with retrieves: burn it over cover, fish a stop-and-go presentation, crawl it along the bottom or rip it off ledges or cover. Every day and every situation is different, and you'll know how to fish it once you get a couple of bass to respond."

Fish have been responding to lipless crankbaits since the 1950s, when Heddon introduced the Sonic. It was shaped similar to today's models, but smaller, and it was touted as a vibrating sinking lure. The lipless concept, however, didn't catch on until the Cordell Spot garnered the bass angler's attention in the 1960s. It was followed shortly thereafter by the Bill Lewis Rat-L-Trap, arguably the most popular lipless lure and the first to bring rattling crankbaits into prominence.

Today, nearly every crankbait manufacturer offers a lipless model, most of which are shaped like a baitfish and contain metallic balls that bang and clang against the plastic shell during the retrieve.

Despite the similarities of these baits, pros say the lures vary greatly in the sounds they emit, and there are days when one sound inexplicably appeals to the fish more than the rattles of another lure.

"Most lipless crankbaits have their own unique sounds, so it pays to carry more than one brand," says Kentucky pro Mike Auten. "I've found that if I am catching fish on a 1/2-ounce Rat-L-Trap in an area and the action slows or stops, I can switch to a different brand in the same size and color and pick up a few more fish, because the sound is a little different."

For example, the Rat-L-Trap has a deeper rattling sound than the Rattlin' Spot, while Rapala's Rattlin' Rap makes less noise than either.

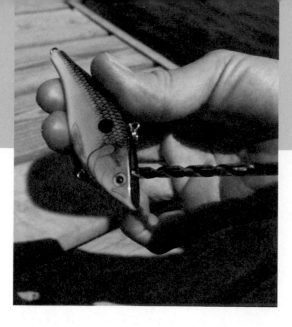

TO ADD WEIGHT to the nose of a Rattlin' Rap, Mike Auten drills a hole in the head and pours in melted Cerrobend to make the lure fall faster and land on its nose.

SHALLOW TECHNIQUES

When Danny Kirk won a tournament on Florida's Lake Toho, he caught several of his quality bass on a chrome/blue back Rat-L-Trap that he yo-yoed over the top of grass in 7 feet of water. He allowed the lure to fall close to the tops of weeds about 5 feet down, then ripped it abruptly each time it touched the weeds.

"When you fish a 'Trap around scattered grass, most of the strikes come when the lure ticks the grass and changes the motion," says the Bartow, Ga., angler. "I've found this yo-yoing method to be really effective in grass, especially in colder water and when the fish aren't overly aggressive."

In contrast, Marty Stone opted for a "slow roll" presentation when he won a tournament on Wheeler Lake in northern Alabama. Stone went to the back of a creek where large schools of baitfish were drawn to fresh water pouring in. The forage fish attracted bass, which roamed through patches of milfoil on a large, 2-foot-deep flat.

Although other anglers fished similar lures nearby, Stone realized the lethargic bass wanted a slow presentation that best resembled the shad. He worked a 1/4-ounce Cordell Rattlin' Spot methodically over the bottom, fishing it far slower than other fishermen were working theirs.

"Everyone thinks that you've got to fish a lipless

crankbait fast, but that wasn't the way these bass wanted it," he explains. "I purposely fished it on a slow retrieve reel. I held my rod tip low and wound it just fast enough to make it wobble. If it caught in the grass, that was OK with me."

"Larger lipless lures would burrow into the grass and were difficult to fish," he recalls. "That's why you've got to get familiar with your lures and choose the one that fits the situation."

Rat-L-Trap spokesman Ken Chaumont says you can slow the retrieve of a lipless lure in shallow water by removing the rear hook and replacing it with a Sampo swivel and tiny willowleaf spinnerbait blade. That feature is built into the Bill Lewis Lures' Spin Trap, but you can modify other brands to perform accordingly.

"You can't use a blade that's too big or you'll kill the action," says Chaumont. "But the small blade gives the bait enough lift that you can fish it slowly over shallow grassy areas."

While a slower retrieve can be important, especially in muddy water, don't assume that it's necessary in clear, cold water, says Texas pro Tommy Martin.

"Lipless crankbaits are the exception to the rule about fishing lures slower in cold water," he adds. "Everywhere I've fished, the fast retrieve has been critical to catching fish on this lure in clear water, even when the water temperature is below 50 degrees."

MAKE SURE you have a good selection of lipless crankbaits in your arsenal. Subtle variations in color or body shape could be the difference in whether or not you get bites.

DEEP WATER PRESENTATIONS

Blaukat says the lipless crankbait can be a good alternative for fishing in areas where the Carolina rig should catch them, but doesn't.

"It's a good backup bait for deep fishing and, yet, a lure most anglers wouldn't consider in that application," he adds. "When fished appropriately, it can trigger reaction strikes from bass that won't bite the subtle, dragging presentation you get from a Carolina rig soft plastic lure."

Auten also uses lipless lures as "drop" baits, providing the cover and structure is appropriate. He alters lures used for this purpose, however, by adding weight to their noses to make them fall more sharply. He drills a 1/8-inch hole into the head above the eyes of a 3/4-ounce Rattlin' Rap or a 1-ounce Spot and fills it with weighted material to make it dive nose first (and faster). Most lipless crankbaits are weighted in the nose, but Auten wants more weight up there in his specialty baits to cause a more dramatic nose-first dive.

He says Rattlin' Raps and Spots have separate chambers, front and back, which are separated by a thin wall of plastic. Rat-L-Traps, he adds, have a more hollow body and are more difficult to weight on the nose.

"You'll probably ruin a few lures in the process, so it takes awhile to get the hang of it," he says. "Make sure that you seal them tightly with epoxy. If water leaks inside, they won't work."

You can use lead to weight the lures, but he prefers a material called "Cerrobend," which is commonly used in tool-and-die shops. Cerrobend

is easier to work with because it has such a low melting point and can be heated with a cigarette lighter.

"A weighted bait sinks fast, and when it hits the bottom, it hits nose first, with the tail riding up," Auten says. "That's part of the attraction."

Obviously, he adds, you can't use these weighted lures where there is a lot of brush because they will snag easily.

"The technique is ideal for shell beds, rock ledges and tapering flats in 7 to 15 feet of water," says Auten, who uses the technique in the summertime on ledges in Kentucky Lake. "Those places also can be fished with diving or lipped crankbaits, but the lipless variety seems to be more productive when you know the fish are keying on gizzard shad."

Auten says he lets the lure hit bottom, then hops it back to the boat, working the rod from a 9 o'clock to 12 o'clock position. Most strikes occur as the bait flutters to the bottom, he adds, so it's important to watch the line as the lure settles to the bottom.

All pros agree that fishermen should spend more time experimenting with lipless lures to determine which presentation is the most effective.

"Most anglers, including a lot of pros, make the mistake of sticking with one brand of lipless lure and fishing it the same way every time," says Martin. "You need to spend time getting familiar with the different brands and learning how they perform in each situation. That can make a difference between catching only a few fish and putting together a big limit."

MOST LIPLESS crankbaits contain large metal BBs in the nose for weight, and smaller ones in the rear for rattling.

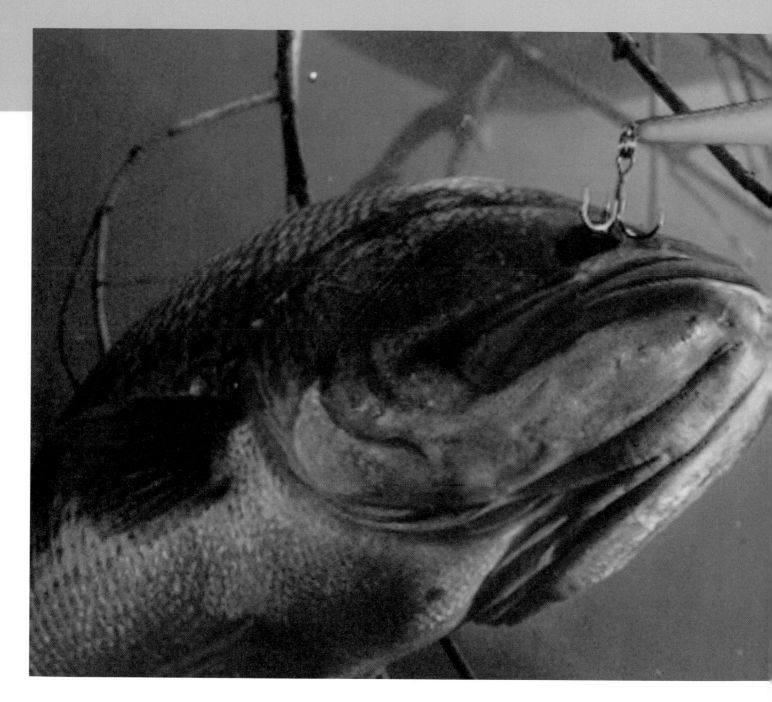

ALTHOUGH THE frantic action of a jerkbait demands the attention of bass, the strike usually occurs on the pause.

JERKBAITS: THE BEST IN THE BOX
The versatility of this bait makes it a favorite

KEVIN VANDAM doesn't hesitate when asked to name his favorite clear water lures. "Jerkbaits," he says emphatically. "When I need to cover a lot of water or I need to stimulate bass to strike, it's the best lure in my box."

The two time Busch B.A.S.S. Angler of the Year from Michigan knows a thing or two about fishing clear water. Most of the lakes he fishes near his home are so clear he can see crawfish moving along the bottom in 10 feet of water.

"A jerkbait is a sight-oriented bait," he notes. "While there are rattles in some brands, it's the visible action of the lure that draws strikes. Obviously, if the fish can't see it because of water clarity or depth, they won't bite it."

FLOATERS VS. SUSPENDERS

Generally, VanDam prefers floating jerkbaits to the suspending or sinking models, although he carries several variations of each style. He usually opts for nonfloaters when the water temperature is below 60 degrees and the fish aren't as active, or if the fish are in water deeper than 8 feet. He also switches to a suspending model after a major cold front passes and the fish are following the floater but not striking it.

"Most manufacturers add weight to the jerkbait to make it suspend or sink," he describes. "Unfortunately, added weight kills some of the side-to-side action that I think is important in warmer water."

He also prefers the standard 4-inch-long version over smaller baits because the bigger lure is more visible and has three sets of treble hooks.

"I will downsize to a Storm Junior ThunderStik or a

VARIOUS BRANDS of jerkbaits may look similar, but their actions can be very different. Anglers should experiment to learn the characteristics of each.

"I experiment with jerkbaits to learn their inherent features," he says. "In the clear water, I can see how bass respond to lure movement and that gives me a big advantage when fishing is tough. I've found that just about any jerkbait will catch fish as long as you apply it to the right conditions."

VanDam believes there are only two times during the year when jerkbaits aren't a good choice: the dog days of summer and the dead of winter. In both seasons, clear water bass tend to live too deep for the shallow running baits to be effective.

Doctoring Jerkbaits

You can convert a floating jerkbait into a sinker by adding weight to the belly of the lure.

"I prefer to drill a hole in the plastic, add a lead insert, then seal the hole with epoxy," says Kevin VanDam. "You can make a Smithwick Rogue run deeper and have good action, but you ruin a lot of baits trying to get it right."

For that reason, the Michigan pro recommends anglers experiment with Storm SuspenDots or SuspenStrips that can be stuck to the bottom or the lure. The weighted, adhesive material can be added or removed without damaging the lure, enabling anglers to fine-tune the sinking or suspending action.

"The balance point of a jerkbait is just ahead of the front treble hook," VanDam explains. "To make the lure suspend horizontally, put SuspenDots near the front of the hook hanger. If you want the lure to dive a little deeper, add the weight closer to the nose. And if you want more side-to-side action, put the weight near the rear." He cautions that adding weight to the nose will reduce tail action and adding it to the rear will reduce running depth.

"Some anglers wrap lead around the hook shaft, but I don't recommend that," he adds. "It hurts the action and will interfere with the hook set."

How Weight Affects Action

1 Adding weight here makes the bait dive deeper.
2 Adding weight here makes the bait suspend horizontally.
3 Adding weight here gives the bait a wider wobble.

natural-looking, Japanese finesse-style model if the fish aren't responding to the standard size," he adds.

VanDam fishes jerkbaits on a slack line by popping the rod tip forward, then immediately allowing it to recoil so that slack forms in the line. He pops the rod four or five times with one revolution of the reel handle, advancing the bait only a couple of inches with each movement. The slack enhances the side-to-side action and prevents the lure from lunging rapidly out of the strike zone.

IF BASS are continually getting hooked on the last treble of your jerkbait, consider slowing down the retrieve, or pausing longer between jerks.

Good floating lures, he adds, wiggle not only when they are pulled forward, but also during the pause portion of the retrieve.

"That's why I think they're more effective during warm months," he offers. "I fish the jerkbait fast, with a lot of short twitches. I don't want the fish to see it sitting still, because they might become suspicious. The lure's shape and action is what fools them into striking."

VanDam, who has helped Strike King develop a line of jerkbaits, suggests anglers experiment in swimming pools with all brands to learn how each one responds to different retrieves.

"A floating Bomber Long A is a bait I like for short, fast twitches because it has a wiggly, darting action," he explains. "Now, if I want to use a bait with a longer pull-and-stop retrieve, I like the Smithwick Rattlin' Rogue."

Most of the time, he prefers plastic lures to ones carved from balsa. Balsa jerkbaits are difficult to cast in wind, they're extremely buoyant and they don't run as deep as plastic lures. VanDam likes balsa baits like the A.C. Shiner or the traditional Rapala, however, for fishing over shallow vegetation, because of their buoyancy.

"Casting distance is important in clear water, so you're really limited in the situations

where you can use balsa jerkbaits effectively," he explains.

Water depth is another consideration. Most floaters dive 4 feet or less while sinking; suspending styles sometimes run as deep as 8 feet. If the water is clear enough, though, a jerkbait can pull fish from well beyond its suspending range.

VanDam proved that at Lake Ontario when he won the 1995 New York Invitational on a suspending Long A. Even though he worked the jerkbait only about 5 feet below the surface, the bigger smallmouth he caught came from water depths ranging from 12 to 18 feet.

"The Long A was ideal because I could draw the smallmouth from a long way in the clear water and, because it suspended, I could keep it in the strike zone longer," he explains. "That allowed the bass time to come get it before the lure reached the surface."

VanDam believes the suspending Long A has the liveliest action of all suspending jerkbaits. He likes Rapala's Husky Jerks, however, in cold water because of their erratic action and the variety of sizes in which they are offered.

BAITCASTING VS. SPINNING

Castability is VanDam's primary concern when deciding the type of equipment to use. He chooses spinning tackle for lighter baits such as the Rattlin' Rogue, A.C. Shiner and small Husky Jerks, and baitcast gear for Long A's or weighted Rogues.

"I use 8- or 10-pound line on spinning and 10 or 12 in most casting situations," he offers. "Heavy line can stifle the action on most jerkbaits, although I've found the Long A can work adequately with heavier line. When I want to work a jerkbait over heavy cover, I'll fish the Long A on line up to 20-pound test."

VanDam believes jerkbaits respond best when fished on low stretch monofilament lines and soft-tip graphite rods. Fiberglass rods may be more forgiving while playing fish, but he says their slow tips deprive the lure of some of its erratic action.

A WORD ABOUT COLOR

Match jerkbait colors to water clarity and the forage. The clearer the water, the more important natural colors become. As a rule, he chooses shad shades in clear water, and clown or firetiger colors in stained water. He sticks to solid colors, like pearl or chartreuse, on cloudy days, because they look more natural without the sunlight.

"I can't emphasize enough the importance of giving the bait a natural appearance," he says. "When fishing jerkbaits in clear water, the right combination of color and action can trigger strikes from bass that would avoid other types of lures."

A JERKBAIT is VanDam's favorite lure to use when coaxing smallmouth from deep, clear water.

INDEX

INDEX